MW00473491

The People

KEY CONCEPTS

Published

The People

Margaret Canovan

polity

Copyright © Margaret Canovan, 2005

The right of Margaret Canovan to be identified as Author of this Work has been asserted in accordance with the UK Copyright, Designs and Patents Act 1988.

First published in 2005 by Polity Press

Polity Press
65 Bridge Street
Cambridge CB2 1UR, UK.

Polity Press
350 Main Street
Malden, MA 02148, USA

All rights reserved. Except for the quotation of short passages for the purpose of criticism and review, no part of this publication may be reproduced, stored in a retrieval system, or transmitted, in any form or by any means, electronic, mechanical, photocopying, recording or otherwise, without the prior permission of the publisher.

ISBN: 0-7456-2821-4
ISBN: 0-7456-2822-2 (pb)

A catalogue record for this book is available from the British Library.

Typeset in 10.5 on 12 pt Sabon
by Servis Filmsetting Ltd, Manchester
Printed and bound in Great Britain by TJ International Ltd, Padstow, Cornwall

The publisher has used its best endeavours to ensure that the URLs for external websites referred to in this book are correct and active at the time of going to press. However, the publisher has no responsibility for the websites and can make no guarantee that a site will remain live or that the content is or will remain appropriate.

Every effort has been made to trace all copyright holders, but if any have been inadvertently overlooked the publishers will be pleased to include any necessary credits in any subsequent reprint or edition.

For further information on Polity, visit our website: www.polity.co.uk

Contents

Acknowledgements

I am indebted to Keele University and the Arts and Humanities Research Board for the research leave that allowed me to start work on this book, and to the Rockefeller Foundation for the month's residency at Bellagio that provided ideal conditions for finishing it. Michael Freeden, Yves Mény, Noel O'Sullivan and Bhikhu Parekh were generous with support and encouragement as referees. Several parts of the book are descended from papers discussed at conferences or seminars where I learned a great deal from those who took part. A few passages have already appeared in a chapter, 'Taking politics to the people: populism as the ideology of democracy', in Y. Mény and Y. Surel (eds), *Democracies and the Populist Challenge* (Basingstoke: Palgrave, 2002, 25–44), and in an article, 'Populism for political theorists', published in *The Journal of Political Ideologies*, 9 (2004) 241–52.

I am grateful to Fergus Millar for a pre-publication copy of his book on *The Roman Republic in Political Thought*. Bernard Yack not only let me read part of his forthcoming book, *Nation and Individual: Contingency, Choice and Community in Modern Political Life,* but also read much of my draft and offered helpful and supportive criticism. Robert Dyson saw a draft of chapter 2 and did his best to lessen my ignorance of Roman and medieval thought. I received helpful responses to early drafts of some chapters from my former colleagues at Keele, notably Andrew Dobson, Rosemary O'Kane and Hidemi Suganami. I owe special debts to John Horton and to April Carter, both of whom read the whole book and responded with incisive criticisms and constructive suggestions. In conclusion, I thank my husband for his unfailing patience and support.

1

Introduction

It is two hundred years since 'We, the people of the United States' bestowed their authority on the American Constitution. In the course of those two centuries the principle that the people's consent is the only basis for legitimate government has become a commonplace. Within contemporary politics, the language of 'the people' is inescapable. Politicians may hail each electoral victory as a popular mandate, but opponents of their policies can call for contentious issues to be given to the people themselves to decide, or even (in the classic populist cry) for political power to be taken from politicians and 'given back to the people'. Outside the politics of stable democracies, more is at stake when 'the people' are invoked. The collapse of Communism in Eastern Europe in 1989 was triggered by massive demonstrations of 'people power' that challenged the credentials of the so-called 'People's Democracies'. 'We are the People', chanted the East German demonstrators in 1989 – we, the protestors, not you, the regime – implying that authority and right were therefore on their side. Most subversive of all is the belief (confirmed by United Nations declarations) that any 'people' has a right to self-determination; in the decade that followed the collapse of Communism bitter wars were fought in the Balkans and elsewhere as rival 'peoples' claimed that right.

Since 'the people' can apparently confer legitimacy on boundaries, constitutions, regimes and policies, all sorts of groups and interests have an incentive to claim that they are or speak for the people. No wonder, then, that such language is as fuzzy as it is familiar. Claims by all and sundry to be the voice of the people blur the notion's meaning – a process that was in fact well under way long before the advent of modern democratic politics. The current ambiguities of 'the people' are a legacy of centuries of use in political controversy. When the seventeenth-century Royalist Sir Robert Filmer wanted to attack the use made of the notion by Charles I's adversaries, he was able even then to point out that, 'What the word people means is not agreed upon' (Filmer 1949: 252). The Parliamentarians and Levellers who used, adapted and extended talk of the sovereign people were themselves drawing on a complex language echoing earlier controversies going back many centuries to the ancient Roman politicians who had claimed the consent of the *populus* for their projects.

Like other terms that have been much contested, 'the people' carries an assortment of meanings, many of them incompatible with one another. Some of these senses are readily translatable between languages, others less so. The English term shares three basic senses with its equivalents in other European languages: the people as sovereign; peoples as nations, and the people as opposed to the ruling elite (what used to be called 'the common people') (Mény and Surel 2000). These are all conceptions of collective political identity, though the collectivities to which they refer are not the same and are all problematic in one way or another. But within the Anglophone discourse that has done much to shape the concerns of modern democratic politics, 'people' (without an article) also refers to human beings as such, individuals in general. Although this use of the term is grammatically separate from more obviously political senses, its meaning colours the other uses, bringing in two extra elements of political ambiguity. In the first place it makes 'the sovereign people' seem like a collection of individuals as well as a collective body; secondly it implies that 'people' and their rights are universal, crossing the boundaries that confine particular 'peoples'. These extra dimensions have confused and enriched Anglo-American traditions of thought and discourse, and this book will therefore be particularly (though not exclusively) attentive to those traditions. Chapter 2 sketches the long history of adaptation through controversy that lies behind 'the people's' present obscurity, setting the scene for the more analytical chapters that follow.

The vagueness of 'the people' is a mark of its political usefulness; captured at different times by many different political causes, it has been stretched to fit their different shapes. But to dismiss it as the empty rhetoric of populist politicians would be a mistake. There are good reasons for 'the people's' obscurities and for trying to clarify these muddy waters. The ambiguities that make the notion so hard to define reflect not only a history of political conflict but also the real issues involved in those conflicts.

'The people's' problems can be conveniently divided into two categories, each with two aspects. There are in the first place issues to do with boundaries, external and internal. How is one 'people' to be distinguished from another, or from people in general? And are 'the people' a part or the whole of the political community? Secondly, what are we to make of the authority of the sovereign people? Can it be exercised, or even clearly conceived? And does it have any basis more solid than myth? The remainder of this introductory chapter summarizes the issues involved.

1 Identifying the People

Who are the 'people' who form the ultimate source of political authority? The obvious answer is perhaps, 'the adult population of each state in the United Nations', but that is much too simple. We cannot even take for granted that a state's external borders correspond to the boundaries of a people, and internally the situation is yet more complex. While usually referring to the polity as a whole, 'the people' as a category has often been narrower than the population – sometimes because it referred to an exclusive group of privileged citizens, but sometimes (conversely and confusingly) because it meant precisely those excluded from that elite, the 'common people'. Externally and internally, the blurred boundaries of the people reflect conflicts and dilemmas that continue to bedevil democratic politics.

Ourselves and Others

The 'peoples' credited with the right to self-determination may at times be defined by existing state boundaries; indeed those who drew up United Nations declarations endorsing that right had in mind decolonization rather than ethnic secession. Much of the notion's force, however, is the plausibility with which it can be used to challenge such boundaries. The most bitterly contested claims to self-determination are those where (it is claimed) frontiers and people do not coincide. In some cases a 'people' is held to extend across an existing border. 'We are the people', the chant of the Leipzig demonstrators in 1989, changed rapidly into 'We are *one* people' – one people with the population of West Germany. In retrospect, many on either side of the old frontier may now be less sure that there was only one German people, but there is no denying that belief in that changed the political map of Europe. In contrast to that unifying conception of the true boundaries of the people, the collapse of Communism in Yugoslavia led rapidly to secessionist movements by minorities claiming to be separate peoples, and thence to civil war and 'ethnic cleansing' of those thought to belong to a different 'people'.

In the German and Yugoslav cases 'people' was understood in ethno-national terms, and there are powerful reasons why this should be so. But republicans and internationalists claim that a self-governing 'people' does not have to fit that pattern. It was in city-states, not nations, that the conception of popular sovereignty was first articulated; more recently, the example of the United States of America has seemed to some to show that a single people with powerful political solidarity is possible in conditions of ethnic diversity. Can the European Union bind its component peoples into a single people, as European visionaries hope? And how can it, or any other polity claiming authority from the people, justify closing its borders against migrants who are themselves people? Can it not be argued that popular sovereignty and self-determination must include all people everywhere? The issues raised by any 'people's' external boundaries are explored in chapter 3.

Part and Whole

Supposing that we could ignore those problems of external definition, it might seem obvious that the people of any particular polity are simply the population inside its borders. Instead this area of membership harbours some of the most curious and significant ambiguities of 'the people'. By immemorial tradition the term (like *populus* and *demos* before it) has meant both the whole political community and some smaller group within it; furthermore, while it has often happened that one group identified as 'the people' was a political elite from which most were excluded, the term 'people' has also been regularly used to denote the excluded lower orders. From the point of view of radicals challenging the existing political order these ambiguities have provided useful leverage. The long struggle for the vote in Britain hinged on claims by the 'common people' that they also were people, indeed the largest part of the true sovereign people (the whole polity) and that they were therefore entitled to join and outvote the privileged political 'people'.

Although universal suffrage has largely put paid both to the notion of the common people and to the old notion of an elite 'people', the elastic internal boundaries of 'the people' still have great political significance. The perennial cry of populists is that power has been stolen from the people by politicians and special interests. Calls to 'give politics back to the people' exploit the ambiguity according to which 'the people' is first understood by contrast with the power-holders (and therefore as something less than the population at large) and then expanded to wield the authority of the sovereign people as a whole. Populists may have a bad name (at any rate in Europe) but their trump card, the belief in popular sovereignty, lies at the heart of democracy itself. How is it, then, that they can be regarded in some circles as anti-democrats, threatening right-wing dictatorship? Should we see them rather as radical democrats, seeking to restore democracy to its true principles? Does populism as a political phenomenon have something to tell us about the complexities of democracy, and especially about the elusive 'people'? These issues will be discussed in chapter 4.

2   The Sovereign People in Action and in Myth

Questions about who 'the people' are will lead us into the darker obscurities explored in chapters 5 and 6, which discuss issues to do with that people's supposed sovereignty. How – if at all – could the people who are the source of legitimate authority actually exercise that ultimate sanction? And what, in any case, is the nature of this authority? Is it (in the strictest sense) mythical?

What prompts these questions is that 'the people' as sovereign appears to refer to two quite different things. On the one hand it refers to something collective, abstract, dignified and mysterious: an entity – 'the British people' or 'We, the people of the United States' – that has a continuous existence and history, transcending and outliving its individual members. On the other hand it also means those individual members themselves, a collection of ordinary, ever-changing people with their separate lives, interests and views. The English language matches this ambiguity with grammatical uncertainty. In English, most collective nouns can take either a singular or a plural verb: 'the team *has* won the trophy' or 'the team *have* lost the match'. In the case of 'people' the plural is more common, perhaps because we also use the word to refer to human beings in general, as in 'people distrust politicians'. Grammatically, we can if we wish say that 'the Polish people *has* a tragic history' but we are just as likely to say that 'the Polish people *have* voted to join the EU'. The issues involved here are not merely linguistic. Although in French and German '*peuple*' and '*Volk*' may be grammatically singular, the problem of relating this collective entity to its collection of individual members is hidden rather than solved.

This problem has two aspects. In the first place, can the notion of the people as the source of political authority have any clear or practical meaning? Are there any circumstances in which we can say that actions by some individual people really do carry the authority of the people as a whole? Secondly, what is it about this people (composed, after all, of ordinary individual people) that makes it authoritative? How large a role in sustaining the notion is played by myths, and do those myths have any solid basis?

The Sovereign People in Action

If 'the sovereign people' refers both to a collection of transitory individuals and to a collective entity that continues over the generations, how are we to understand the relation between collection and collectivity? Crucially, what does it mean to say that the people have/has exercised their/its authority? Elected politicians claim that they represent the whole people and can speak and act on their behalf, but the appeal of populist movements is built on voters' reluctance to believe that. Chapter 5 examines the issue from two complementary angles. Can we in the first place make sense in theoretical terms of the notion that individual people form an authoritative collective people? There are plenty of other collective bodies – from firms to football clubs – that seem to be able to possess and exercise powers in a comprehensible and effective way; why is it so much harder to give a clear account of 'the people' as a collectivity?

The second aspect of this problem is less theoretical, more practical and institutional. Supposing that we can form a clear idea of an authoritative 'people' that is both a continuing whole and a collection of individuals, can we point to actions in which its authority has been exercised? Do general elections transfer that authority to politicians? Do referendums reveal the will of the sovereign people? Might popular consent be more authentically revealed by the outcome of a public debate on some issue – or perhaps in the mass demonstrations dubbed 'people power'? Should we perhaps conclude that popular authorization can never be given adequate institutional form because it belongs to a more fluid aspect of politics, in which brief episodes of popular mobilization are encapsulated in myths? Chapter 6 goes on to pursue the elusive sovereign people into this murky region.

Myths of Popular Authority

In today's political struggles activists of all stripes are anxious to claim popular authorization for their cause. The pragmatic reasons for this are obvious enough – everyone wants the voters on their side. But political discourse seems to imply that the people have authority as well as votes, and this is more puzzling. For what is there about the people to make them the ultimate political authority?

If we think of 'the people' simply as the population – a collection of ordinary ignorant human beings – then their claim to be regarded as the fount of political legitimacy is not obvious, as anti-democrats since Plato have pointed out. It is possible to make a powerful negative case for the involvement of the general population in decision-making, on the grounds that this can limit rulers' abuse of power by making them take notice of as many interests as possible. But that hard-headed negative argument is not prominent in the political discourse of popular sovereignty. That has always had a more positive tone, asserting or implying that the attribution of sovereign authority to the people is more than a prudential device; that it is indeed a matter of right, from which good results can be expected to follow. If we consider the enthusiasm that greeted the outbreak of people power in Eastern Europe in 1989, or the pathos of the first post-Apartheid election in South Africa, we must recognize that the notion of the sovereign people is credited with a quality that lifts it far above people as ordinary human beings. It is that mysterious quality that encourages so many to claim that they are the true voice of the people, and this special quality finds expression in myths.

Chapter 6 examines myths of past foundation and future redemption by the people, and the way in which such myths colour our view of popular movements happening before our eyes. The second part of the chapter considers how we should regard that mythic sovereign people. Should we take a robustly cynical view, treating the notion simply as a manipulative device? Plenty of supporting evidence can be found for this; if we ask why anyone continues to be taken in, a cynic might point to the human craving for moral certainty, which is so insistent that the collapse of other more or less mythical authorities – Custom, God, King and Party – makes us fall back on a mythical People simply to find authority somewhere. But a less dismissive response might suggest that our familiar myths of the People as founder and redeemer of polities may have rather more substance than that. If there were a kernel of truth hidden in the myths, it might be a truth about the basis of political power and political community. On that view, the hidden truth of the myth is that ordinary individual people do have the potential (however rarely exercised) to mobilize for common action. On occasion, such grass–roots mobilizations generate enough power to bring down a regime; more rarely, they sometimes manage to make a fresh start and to lay the foundations of a lasting political community. Seen in that light, it might be the rarity, contingency and brevity of such moments that makes popular authority so hard to pin down and 'the sovereign people' so mysterious and vague a notion. According to that account, the people as a source of action and authority is more often potential than actual, haunting the political imagination and tempting political entrepreneurs but exasperating tidy-minded students of politics.

Whatever the persuasiveness of that analysis there is no denying that 'the people' has a long history within political myth, political rhetoric and political theory. The next chapter attempts a brief survey of some of the main themes within that history.

2

'The People' and its Past

The conceptual language of 'the people' is rich but bewilderingly ambiguous, and if we are to make sense of its resonances we need some degree of historical depth. Anything approaching a full-scale history of the notion is beyond the scope of this book, but a more modest and selective attempt will be made here to sketch some of the political battles fought in terms of 'the people' and to trace the strands of meaning that diverge and converge through them. Most of the chapter will be concerned with the Anglophone discourse of the period (beginning with the English revolutions of the seventeenth century) when traditional sources of political legitimacy were challenged in the name of popular sovereignty and 'the people' came to embody a comprehensive radical project. Despite the universal scope of its claims that radical project took different forms in different languages and political cultures; *peuple*, *popolo* and *Volk* are not equivalent to 'people' or to one another, and their separate stories cannot be told here.

In order to understand any of those traditions of discourse, however, we need to start further back, with the Roman *populus* from which the political language of 'people' is descended. It is the Roman heritage that will be stressed here rather than the Greek. We are familiar with histories of democracy that start from ancient Athens, but have to pass rapidly over a long era of sacred monarchy when 'democracy' was not honoured as an ideal. As their authors point out, that term still had derogatory overtones at the time of the American and French Revolutions. By contrast, the language of *populus*/people was kept alive for two millennia by the massive inheritance of Roman history, law and literature, which was still a source of political wisdom for the founding fathers of the American Constitution. Within that Roman heritage, *'populus*/people' had favourable connotations that 'democracy' lacked. The *populus* had been at the heart of the Roman Republic and it left behind a complex legacy.

The story told in this chapter therefore begins with the *populus Romanus* and traces the adaptations of that notion which allowed popular sovereignty to become part of the ideological discourse of monarchy, first as a buttress for kingship and later as a justification for rebellion. The seventeenth-century Englishmen who struggled against their Stuart kings drew on that inheritance to develop theories of popular sovereignty that were further adapted and acted out a century later, above all in America. Despite the unparalleled drama of the French Revolution, I shall argue that an investigation into the contemporary resonances of 'the people' needs to pay particular attention to the legacy of the *American* Revolution, variously developed in Britain and in the USA itself. The narrative provided below is unavoidably selective, simplified and compressed. I hope that it may nevertheless convey something of the historical depth and complexity of the forms of thought and discourse centred on 'the people'.

1   Prelude in Rome: The People in Action

Who or what was the Roman *populus*? One of its images is familiar to us from Shakespeare's Roman plays: as the mob in the forum so easily swayed first by Brutus and then by Mark Antony; the 'beast with many heads' castigated by Coriolanus. (Shakespeare 1967: 140; cf. Horace 1994: 57) Within the mixed constitution of republican Rome power was shared between elected consuls, the Senate and popular assemblies, obliging aristocratic contenders for power to seek plebeian support (Lintott 1999). '*Populus*' often referred to these plebeian citizens by contrast with the patrician class, and *populares* were politicians who made a point of cultivating them and playing to the crowd (Millar 1998: 124). This is one of the meanings of *populus* that was carried over from Latin to English, though with a difference that would eventually be important. Whereas the plebeian *populus* was a defined class of *citizens*, inferior to patricians but privileged by comparison with slaves, the English 'common people' would include all the lower orders.

But this was only one aspect of the Roman *populus*. While the term could refer to the less exalted part of the polity, it could also mean the polity as a whole, including all the parts of the mixed constitution (Lintott 1999: 72).[1] Even the *populus* as crowd in the forum were transfigured when they formally assembled in their tribes to pass laws in the *comitia*, (Lintott 1999: 42–3), for they did so as representatives of the *populus Romanus*, a collective entity that transcended specific individuals, classes and generations. This *populus*, in other words, meant the whole political community.[2] As Cicero (not one of the *populares*) put it, what the *res publica* itself amounts to is the *res populi*, that is, the affairs of the *populus* in its inclusive and corporate sense (Cicero 1999: xxxvii, 18). It was this inter-generational, quasi-national *populus* that had conquered an empire and enacted the glorious history recorded by Livy (Livius 1974: 1; cf Feldherr 1998: 30, 218). That territorial expansion had by the end of the Republic generated an expanded *populus Romanus universus*, most of it too far from Rome to take part in the sovereign assemblies of the people. But Cicero claimed that what makes a people is agreement on common law and common interests, an interpretation that helped this wider *populus* to take conceptual form (Cicero 1999: 18). If it was 'Romanness' rather than the active exercise of political power that was the mark of the Roman people, then that people could gradually turn into a much larger and vaguer political community, no longer tied specifically to a city-state or to its republican institutions.

The political practice of the Roman Republic therefore left behind a complex legacy. It was a strikingly successful example of a specific and unusual form of government: a mixed government, but one in which the *populus* in the sense of a large body of plebeian citizens held and exercised substantial political power.[3] But it also left behind two more abstract conceptions of *populus*. One was specific and geographically bounded; the medieval monarchies from whose realms European nation-states grew would later be able to draw on the memory of the Roman people as a specific, collective political entity that had generated and exercised extraordinary power across space and over time. In this sense, *populus* meaning polity would become applicable to a kingdom like England or France (Black 1992: 15; Reynolds 1984: 250–60). For many centuries after the end of the Republic, however, it was a different language of *populus* that was dominant, one much broader and vaguer, as the *populus Romanus* became identified first with the civilized world and then (once Rome had become Christian) with Christendom. Taking up Cicero's notion that what makes a people is agreement on what is right, St Augustine argued in the fourth century that the only true 'people' is the people of God's City (Augustine 1998: 78–80), a suggestion elaborated by later churchmen. But 'Christian' was readily equated with 'Roman' in its extended sense, so that the *populus Dei*, members of the *Respublica Christiana*, could (at any rate to some) seem more or less interchangeable with the *populus Romanus*.

In terms of political power there was an enormous gulf between grand abstractions of this kind and that active Roman people whose support had once been courted by Roman aristocrats. With hindsight, however, the Romans' most significant legacy to subsequent political conceptions of the sovereign people was perhaps the tenuous connection that Roman Imperial lawyers managed to find between the concrete, narrow *populus* of republican practice and its abstract, inflated successors. The key point here is that the end of the Roman Republic was not clear cut; the institutional forms of a self-governing city-state lingered on long after military dictatorship over a vast empire had become the reality. Though master of Rome, Augustus exercised powers legally conferred on him by the Roman popular assembly and Senate, and later emperors continued to go through the pantomime of election and the delegation of popular power. This legal formality was incorporated into the body of Roman law as the *lex regia*, according to which the sovereign power exercised by the emperor was derived by delegation from the Roman people (Homo 1929). Piling fiction upon fiction and drawing on the expansion and transmutation of the *populus Romanus* already mentioned, Charlemagne's German successors as Holy Roman Emperors would later be able to claim a parallel legitimacy, on the grounds that the Roman people were (somehow) represented by the seven German princes whose privilege it was to elect the emperor (Ullmann 1965: 145).

The remarkable political elasticity of the language of 'people' can therefore claim a very long history. One illustration of this is that the very *lex regia* that had been designed to legitimize absolute power turned out in the longer run to provide conceptual tools for popular resistance. As reinterpreted by lawyers in the late Middle Ages (Canning 1996: 8–9, 170; Black 1992: 139) this piece of legal fiction was to become a crucial source for later conceptions of popular sovereignty, because it carried the seed of an enormously fruitful idea. This was the idea of *indirect* authorization, the notion that (even in forms of government that were very far indeed from being democratic) emperors and kings nevertheless somehow derived their power from the people. It was the very vagueness of such language that allowed it to be developed as it was.[4] If the only meaning of popular sovereignty had been the literal, direct exercise of political power by a clearly defined body of citizens (as exemplified in the assemblies of the Roman Republic), then the notion would have had no more relevance to the mainstream politics of kings and emperors than did the Athenian concept of democracy. But the tradition of the *lex regia* offered a theoretical possibility of eroding the boundary between 'popular governments' and others by implying that *all* government could be seen as drawing legitimacy from the people. Within the predominantly theocratic culture of the early Middle Ages this was a very small seed, but one that would later show spectacular potential for growth.

To sum up this section then, the notion of the sovereign people decended from Rome in the form of a double legacy; two distinct conceptual inheritances that went their separate ways for many hundreds of years.

The Republican Legacy of the People in Action

This was the memory of a specific and unusual form of government, the possession of a collective people constituted by a specific, exclusive body of citizens. Despite being a source of inspiration and imitation for some down to the time of the

French Revolution, during the centuries when politics was overwhelmingly monarchical it had little practical relevance outside a few city-states.

The Legacy of the *Lex Regia*: The People in Reserve

Though inconspicuous to begin with, the more significant legacy of Rome turned out to be the notion that 'the people' in some much less determinate sense are the source of *all* legitimate government, even that by emperors and kings. Instead of requiring a special and very rare form of government, popular authorization lies behind all forms, even those that seem most distant from popular power. One implication is that popular consent does not in itself do anything to mandate popular *government* – an implication later pressed with considerable relish by Thomas Hobbes (Hobbes 1983: 151). But this vague and apparently unsatisfactory notion turned out to be capable of development on two fronts.

There was in the first place (in contrast to the practical clarity of republican rule) a fog of vagueness about the relation between the present ruler and his supposed authorization by the people. Often envisaged as a once-and-for-all surrender of power at some time in the past, this could be elaborated into a popular authority left in reserve for use in rare emergencies; then into power to hold the king to account; then into a sovereign right to establish a new constitution, and eventually into a claim for continuous popular self-government.

Furthermore, the notion of the people itself and of how it might take action entirely lacked the definition and clarity of republican practice, within which it was necessary to know precisely who was and who was not part of the *populus*.[5] Gradually interpreted as referring to the people of each separate realm, it did in the course of time acquire geographical boundaries narrower than the whole of Christendom (Reynolds 1984: 250–2, 256). Sociologically, however, it was able to remain foggy for much longer, because until at least the seventeenth century 'the people' was understood as a transgenerational corporate entity with natural representatives in the shape of magnates and community leaders. For many centuries, being an ordinary member of this corporate people therefore implied nothing at all by way of political rights or responsibilities. Even the 'common people' could be regarded as in some sense part of it – a fuzzy inclusiveness eased in England by an early sense of national peoplehood.

The next two sections are concerned with the gradual elaboration and clarification of this foggy notion of the people in reserve, up to the point where (converging at last with the adapted legacy of Roman republicanism) a new version of the people in action emerged in America.

2   The People in Reserve: From Shadow to Substance

Knowledge of Roman law was recovered in Western Europe by the twelfth century, and the *lex regia* with it. The notion that royal authority was in some sense derived from a corporate *populus* fitted comfortably enough with the medieval monarch's customary and pragmatic need to consult those whose support he could not do without (Reynolds 1995: 380–1). But hindsight can easily exaggerate the importance of popular legitimation within a political culture that was in fact strongly theocratic. For many centuries sacred monarchy and papal authority were the main competitors; the idea of popular authorization was brought into contention simply as a reinforcement in the struggle waged by emperors, kings and ecclesiastical councils against papal claims. Even in the later Middle Ages, after the revival of Aristotle's philosophy had given secular rulers promising new territory on which to fight their battles for legitimacy, those who elaborated the idea tended to be much more interested in anti-papalist struggles than in how the *populus* had actually authorized rulers (Black 1992: 65–71; Canning 1996: 157–8; Tierney 1982: 58–9). By the end of the fifteenth century, nevertheless, repeated references to the people as the ultimate source of power had made the idea almost a commonplace. Who the people in question actually *were* remained entirely unclear; furthermore, the commonplace did not imply that kings were necessarily accountable to the people, still less that the latter could exercise sovereignty themselves (Dunbabin 1988: 515, 519, though cf. Skinner 1978: II 122, 130–3). Within the (predominantly Latin) literature on Natural

Law that developed from the sixteenth century, a similarly abstract notion of popular authorization would be used to support monarchy for several centuries more (Tuck 1991: 519–20).

It took a different set of religious quarrels to turn these commonplaces into the doctrine that kings could actually be accountable to the people: the religious struggles set off by the Protestant Reformation in the sixteenth century. Faced with rulers committed to the wrong version of Christianity, Protestant and Catholic writers put forward parallel theories justifying resistance on the ground that power was derived from the people. Protestant resistance theory was most fully articulated by French Huguenots after the St Bartholomew's Day massacre of Protestants in 1572. Its most notable expression, the *Vindiciae contra Tyrannos* of 1579, argued that kings rule by the authority of the people and for the sake of the people's welfare and that their authority is therefore conditional. If the king breaks his contract with the people, the latter have the right to resist. The author assumed that the people of the realm in question form a collectivity with natural representatives who can act on behalf of the whole (Skinner 1978: II 331; Black 1980: 157–8; cf. Wootton 1986: 49). This assumption was regularly made within resistance theory, though a few authors on each side made themselves notorious by arguing that any individual is justified in assassinating a tyrant (Kingdom 1991; Salmon 1991). On the Catholic side, the best-known defence of rebellion and tyrannicide was put forward in 1599 by the Spanish Jesuit, Juan de Mariana, who argued that kings were established by the people and could therefore be removed by them under certain circumstances. While the proper authority to remove a tyrant was the assembly of the realm, any individual was entitled to do so by assassination (Skinner 1978: II 346).

In an age when order depended on stable monarchy, the anarchic potentialities of the doctrine of popular authorization were alarming, leading many to reject it in favour of the divine right of kings. In any case, even those who accepted resistance theory in the sixteenth century thought of recourse to the people as an emergency measure rather than as a continuous exercise of popular oversight, still less as popular government. A different series of political crises prompted the extension of resistance theory in that direction. It was in England and its American offshoots that these crises occurred, from the Civil War of the mid-seventeenth century to the Glorious Revolution of 1688–9 and thence to the American Revolution of the late eighteenth century.

Up to this point in the story of the *populus*/people, the literature considered has been in Latin, the common possession of educated Western Europeans, but out of reach of the common people in England and elsewhere. England in the early seventeenth century might in fact have seemed an unlikely place to spawn sensationally radical developments. The country had been fortunate to avoid the full-scale religious civil wars that were still raging elsewhere in Europe, while support for stable monarchy as a bulwark of peace and order was actually strengthened by the Gunpowder Plot of 1605 (Wootton 1986: 27–30). But England also had a complex constitutional and linguistic heritage on which a new politics of 'the people' could be built. Constitutionally, there was a long-standing tradition that English kings ruled with occasional help from Parliament, and especially that new taxes required the assent of the Commons. While there was little clarity about the precise constitutional relationship between king and Parliament on the one hand, or Parliament and people on the other, it was commonly assumed that Parliament as a whole (King, Lords and Commons) represented the realm as a whole. Summing up this tradition in 1583, Sir Thomas Smith claimed in *De Republica Anglorum* that every Englishman was actually or virtually present when Parliament met, and could therefore be said to consent to its actions (Pitkin 1967: 246).

Constitutionally, therefore, there was scope for identifying the people either with their elected representatives in the Commons or with Parliament as a whole – or, alternatively, as a people in reserve separate from either of these. Linguistically, meanwhile, 'the people' was already a familiar term within English political discourse, with many different senses, one of them unique to English. Like *populus*, 'people' meant both the whole collectivity of the realm and its lower part, the 'common people' (who were not to be confused with the country gentlemen and burgesses who sat in the House of Commons). It also meant *a* people in the sense of one specific collectivity among others, a nation. Even before the Reformation many Englishmen had shared the belief that the English were a specially favoured people with uniquely excellent laws and customs, among them the parliamentary heritage.[6] The Reformation gave that national peoplehood a huge boost, encouraging Protestant Englishmen – such as the cleric who told his flock that 'God is English' – to believe that they were a chosen people with a God-given destiny (Greenfeld 1992: 60; cf. Pocock 1975: 337, 345). This idea of chosen peoplehood was derived from an amalgamation of biblical and Roman traditions, and the Franks had (with papal encouragement) adopted a similar notion long before the English (Folz 1974: 79; Canning 1996: 18, 49, 55). In England, however, common membership of a national people did do something to bridge the gulf between the common people and the political class, reinforcing an inclusive understanding of the people as polity.

More speculatively, this national reinforcement of the sense of *collective*, trans-generational peoplehood may have been politically important at a time when religious, economic and intellectual developments were beginning to emphasize individual rather than collective identity: in religion, the responsibility of the individual for his own salvation; in the economy, the spread of market relationships; in Natural Law theory, the increasing tendency to trace societies to individuals in a state of nature. It is a peculiarity of 'people' in English, unlike the Latin *populus* and its other European derivatives, that it unites collective and individual senses. Not only do the collective senses of the term regularly take plural as well as singular verbs (so that it is more natural to say 'the English people are up in arms' than to say 'the English people is up in arms'), but 'people' in English also has a purely individual (though also universal) meaning, referring to human beings as such. Against this linguistic background, the idea of the sovereign people could be imagined in a number of guises once the Civil War focused attention upon it. Besides the nightmare vision of the common people let loose (Hill 1974) it could appear also as an incoherent but appealing amalgam[7] of the *national* people with its proud inheritance of law and *individual* people, equal human souls before God.

3 Civil War to American Revolution: The English People in Rebellion

The Roman legacy of the *lex regia* had made possible the notion of the people as an authority in reserve, a resource to be drawn on in an emergency rather than a power continually present. A similar pattern of falling back on the people can be observed in both the English Civil War and the American Revolution. In both cases the quarrel was initially understood as a matter of constitutional law, concerning the respective rights of king and Parliament in the first case and of Parliament and colonies in the second. In both cases, however, the less powerful side fell back on to the ground of popular sovereignty, drawing on but extending ideas already widely available. The Americans were able to make use of a powerful battery of arguments developed during the English Civil War and its sequel, the Revolution of 1688/9, though (as we shall see later) what they did with those ideas created something new, the characteristically modern understanding of the sovereign people.

The century and a half between the first stirrings of Civil War in England and the establishment of the US Constitution are so rich in debates about the people that a sequential survey is impossible here. All I shall attempt is to sketch the elaboration during this period of two strands of thought that may be seen as a succession of answers to two connected questions. Logical and chronological sequences do not necessarily coincide; the Levellers were more radical in the 1640s than American Loyalists were in the 1770s, while opponents of popular sovereignty like Sir Robert Filmer could see its subversive potentialities from the start of the period. Over the long term, however, radical ideas gradually came to seem commonplace. In summary, the two questions and their successive answers are as follows.

1   *What does the notion that power stems from the people mean in practical terms?*
    We can trace a drift from recourse to the people only as an emergency measure, first to a strong doctrine of royal accountability to the people, then to the right of the people to remake the constitution, and eventually to

something like a programme for actual popular government.

2   *Who are the people, and how can they act?*
The long-term drift here is from a collective national people represented by natural leaders, to the people as the adult male population of the nation.

The Meaning of Popular Authorization

Resistance theory had turned the medieval commonplace that the people were the ultimate source of legitimate authority into the firmer position that any specific king owes his authority to the specific collective people of his realm, who can in the last resort take back that authority. The people are always there in reserve as the collective recipient of power when ordinary government has failed. It was in those terms that moderate Whigs understood the 1688 Revolution in England, when James II supposedly 'abdicated' after breaking his contract with the people (Ashcraft 1986: 559). Even when it was held to justify rebellion, this reserve capacity of the people was usually thought of as defensive and restorative (Tierney 1982: 80). In 1688 as in 1640 the crisis arose because (in the eyes of his opponents) the king had taken the initiative, breaking his commitments, attacking England's constitution and invading the people's rights. Power therefore returned to the collective people so that they could restore the status quo and vindicate their original rights (whether thought of as the 'rights of Englishmen', as 'natural rights', or as a conflation of the two). It is true that the execution of Charles I allowed a small group of radicals to experiment with constitutional innovations (Pocock 1992: xi), while their successors insisted in 1689 and throughout the eighteenth century on the right of the people to change their constitution as they saw fit. But although such ideas gradually became more acceptable, mainstream opinion continued to defer to the authority of tradition, giving a conservative gloss to most assertions of popular authority.

Even quite radical assertions of popular sovereignty did not necessarily imply popular *rule*. Monarchy was still the normal form of government, even if assisted and limited by

Parliament. Almost all of those who insisted on the ultimate authority of the people (including John Locke) continued to assume that what was at issue was the relation between king and people and the extent to which the former could when necessary be made accountable to the latter. For a classically-minded minority, memories of Roman republicanism encouraged attempts to discard inherited institutions and devise a new republican order, but until the American Revolution ideas of this kind were only an undercurrent (Robbins 1959; Pocock 1975). More typical, being more in tune with prevailing conservatism and national pride, was the gradual reinterpretation of the ancient English constitution. It came to be seen less as a monarchy with limits and more as a version of the mixed constitution so often praised by classical writers, with authority shared between King, Lords and Commons (Gordon 1737: 175; Blackstone 2001: 36–8). Just how the components of this mixed constitution were related to the people remained unclear. Within the House of Commons the people could in some sense be said to be present. On the other hand, King, Lords and Commons together were collectively regarded as representatives of the people, and the eighteenth-century saw the establishment as orthodox legal doctrine of the theory that (on behalf of the people) Parliament as a whole wields absolute sovereign power. Each of these legal fictions was open to challenge in the name of the sovereign people in reserve.

Who are the People, and How can they Act?

As 'the people' emerged from its shadowy existence somewhere in the mists of time and began to take on some features of active sovereignty, this further question became more pressing. We have seen that in resistance theory the people of a particular realm were assumed to form a collectivity with natural leaders through whom it could take action when necessary. Perhaps it had estates of the realm, a Parliament of some kind; if not, the nobles, gentlemen and civic big-wigs who would make up such estates could be regarded as the people's representatives. This theory was classically restated by Edmund Burke at the time of the French Revolution, in the course of his retrospective vindication (in his *Appeal from the New to the Old Whigs*) of the Revolution of 1688/9 (Burke 1834: 524–6). As an account of the activity of the aristocratically-led English 'people' in the Glorious Revolution it was not wholly implausible; Burke knew from his own experience within the profoundly hierarchical and deferential world of eighteenth-century England that a small group of inter-married landowners, each speaking for his own 'people', could sometimes be quite plausibly mistaken for the people of England.

But although the success of the 1689 Revolution settlement might appear to vindicate that interpretation, discussions of 'the people' were haunted by skeletons that had escaped from the cupboard during the Civil War. Identifying the people's natural representatives was not always so easy, nor could the common people always be swept under the carpet of virtual representation. During their struggle with Charles I, members of Parliament had initially taken for granted that they themselves were for all practical purposes 'the people' (Morgan 1988: 64–5). Royalists could and did challenge this pretension on the grounds that Parliament as a whole, including the King, was the true representative of the people, but Charles' opponents had some warrant in tradition for thinking as they did: they were elected according to traditional forms, and they were members of the landowning classes, men of weight in the country. The notion that popular sovereignty might grant power to the grass roots was at first simply a *reductio ad absurdam* (Wootton 1986: 46–8). Within a few years, however, the Levellers had come forward to identify the people with the mass of freeborn Englishmen, most of them common people: 'the hobnails, clouted shoes, the private soldiers, the leather and woollen aprons, and the laborious and industrious people of England' (Wootton 1991: 413; Sharp 1998). Meanwhile royalist polemicists like Sir Robert Filmer subjected the notion of popular authority to a lucid and withering critique. Either 'the people' means every single individual in the country at every moment in time, or else it is just a convenient cloak for the pretensions to power of conspirators of all kinds (Filmer 1949: 252, 226).[8] Most likely it means letting loose against order and property that many-headed monster, the common people (Hill 1974).

For many gentlemen of the propertied and political classes in England the experience of the Civil War was an awful warning of the dangers of toying with any notion of active popular sovereignty. It is easy to understand why in 1683, during a crisis over the succession to Charles II, the doctrine that 'all civil authority is derived originally from the people' was condemned by the Tory University of Oxford (Wootton 1986: 38). Despite the worrying prospect of rule by the Catholic and despotically-inclined James II, there were plenty of Tory pamphleteers to point back to the Levellers and claim that what was at stake was 'the sovereignty of the rabble' (Ashcraft 1986: 298). Worries about how far down society 'the people' might extend troubled many of those who eventually found themselves supporting the 1688 Revolution, encouraging them to accept the fiction that James had 'abdicated' rather than to understand their rebellion in terms of the strong theory of popular authority put forward by John Locke (Wootton 1993: 11–12; Ashcraft 1986: 572; Morgan 1988: 111–12).

Locke's *Second Treatise of Civil Government*, published in 1690 just after the Revolution, is a milestone in the development of the doctrine of popular sovereignty. Just what Locke was up to remains a source of dispute among scholars (cf. Ashcraft 1986; Wootton 1993; Marshall 1994), but the effect of his book (aided by his fame as a philosopher) was to put into circulation a remarkably radical account of what popular sovereignty meant. Whatever his intentions may have been, on the face of it he defended a position that had been treated as the *reductio ad absurdam* by Filmer and other Tories: popular sovereignty, with the sovereign people taken to be a majority of (adult, male) individual people – a majority that must surely consist of the common people (Locke 1964: 367, 372, 385, 398, 426, 445; cf. Ashcraft 1986: 584; Marshall 1994: 276).

The net effect of the Revolution Settlement on eighteenth-century English politics was therefore to give respectability to a range of very different interpretations of the sovereignty of the people, varying from the complacently hierarchical to the subversively radical. At the complacent end of the Whig spectrum, the aristocratic monarchy appeared as a classically mixed constitution that was a unique English inheritance from the mists of time, the possession of a national people that was fuzzily inclusive of the common people, though represented in

Parliament by its natural leaders in the propertied classes. At the other end, not clearly distinguished from this (for were not all those who celebrated the Revolution Whigs of a sort?) were understandings of the people and their powers that were much more majoritarian, individualistic, radical and activist. It was the American Revolution that separated the one from the other and brought the radical interpretation to fruition (Bailyn 1967). It is nevertheless instructive to sample English political opinion just before that crucial break.

In the years before the American crisis there was mounting criticism in England of royal influence in the House of Commons, purchased by bribing MPs with royal 'pensions' and 'places' in government offices. When 'Country' polemicists denounced corruption of Parliament by the Court and warned of the imminent death of English liberty, appeals to popular sovereignty mingled in their arguments with idealization of the immemorial English Constitution and parallels with the demise of the Roman Republic. A good place to look for understandings of the people that were widely shared in England and in the American colonies is James Burgh's three fat volumes of *Political Disquisitions*, published in 1774–5. Burgh is revealing precisely because he was not an original thinker but a widely read author whose work reflects ideas that were generally available at the time (Butterfield 1949: 259–63; Bonwick 1977: 75; Bailyn 1967: 41). Though based on 'revolution-principles' hallowed by the settlement of 1689 (Burgh 1971: I 200) his book illustrates three important shifts in the notion of the sovereign people that were about to be acted out in America.

In the first place, despite Burgh's continual references to the defence and recovery of England's ancient constitution, a more forward-looking, activist conception of popular sovereignty mingles with the traditional defensive conception. Burgh makes a point of asserting the right of the people to give themselves an entirely new constitution if they choose to do so (Burgh 1971: I 221, III 277–99).

Secondly, although Burgh is (in traditional style) prompted to write by a sense of emergency – fear that the English people are about to lose their freedom to absolute monarchy – his conception of popular sovereignty goes far beyond an emergency resource or a mere check on royal rule. His sovereign people are continuously present in the country and expect to be able to control their own affairs through the House of Commons – 'the *people's* house, where the *people's* deputies meet to do the *people's* business' and ought to do so under strict instructions from their constituents (Burgh 1971: I 14). So vivid and concrete is his sense of who the people are and how they can act that he calls on them to defend their freedom by mobilizing, parish by parish and county by county and to form themselves into a 'Grand National Association for Restoring the Constitution' that would represent the people more authentically than the corrupt Parliament could claim to do (Burgh 1971: III 428).

Thirdly, within the framework of a traditionally hierarchical picture of the people, Burgh ambiguously widens it to include the majority. When he talks about 'the power of the people, guided, limited, and directed by men of property' (Burgh 1971: III 426) he assumes (as so many even of his aristocratic Whig contemporaries did, until the French Revolution upset their expectations) that the common people will defer to their betters (Butterfield 1949: 226). Nonetheless, he argues in favour of universal male suffrage (Burgh 1971: I 37) and insists that it is the *majority* of the people that is sovereign, going so far as to add, 'for whatever the majority desire, it is certainly lawful for them to have, unless they desire what is contrary to the laws of God' (Burgh 1971: III 429).

One explanation of Burgh's serene radicalism no doubt lies in his assumption that the people share a single common interest, and that the political contest is simply between the forces of a corrupt Court on the one hand and 'the body of the independent people on the other' (Burgh 1971: III 449). He died in 1775, just too early to see the more radical of his ideas put into practice in America, where rebels proceeded to give a demonstration of the people in action.

4 We the People: The American Revolution and its Significance

Within the story told in this chapter, the importance of the American Revolution can scarcely be overestimated. In the course of that revolution 'the people' moved out into the limelight, and all the different senses of the term merged into a single political project. The Roman Imperial legacy of the *sovereign people* in reserve was reunited with the Roman Republican legacy of *popular government*, including a political role for the *common people*. The *people as nation* claimed their right to self-rule as a special, distinct collectivity – but did so in terms that linked nation, republic and sovereignty to *people in general*, the bearers of universal natural rights. Last but not least, the Revolution established a resonant and enduring *myth of the sovereign people* in action. This complex cluster of ideas and phenomena needs closer examination.

From People in Reserve to Constituent Sovereign

The Declaration of Independence can in a sense be read as the culmination of traditional resistance theory. The unfortunate George III is cast as the tyrant whose misdeeds have forced the sovereign people to reclaim their ultimate authority. But that backward-looking, restorative mood was only a preliminary. In their state constitutions and in the US Constitution itself, a mobilized people apparently exercised sovereignty by establishing entirely new institutions, replacing the authority of antiquity with the authority of present popular consent (Morgan 1988: 122; Hamilton et al. 1886: 135, 552). Both moves, the rebellion and the constitution-making, relied on the assumption (made explicit in *The Federalist*) that there *was* a united people able to take collective action (Hamilton et al. 1886: 135, 552). In face of deep conflicts of interest and loyalty, that assumption was hazardous (Morgan 1988: 267), and yet the outcome seemed to excuse its boldness. Instead of dissolving into anarchy or generating military dictatorship, a broadly-based movement managed to mobilize, generate leaders to act for it, win the war and establish new institutions, visibly acting as a people (Beer 1993: 329). One of the striking features of this mobilization was that it included the (male, white) common people. Constant tensions between classes (Bailyn 1967: 288: Commager 1951: 210) did not prevent the success of the revolution or the establishment of the constitution.

Popular Government

The phenomenon that needs to be underlined, however, goes beyond the reassertion of sovereignty by a relatively inclusive people, and beyond even the establishment by that sovereign people of a new constitution. The most momentous novelty was that, at a time when the normal form of polity was some variant of aristocratic monarchy, the Americans established 'popular government'. Ever since some medieval Italian city-states had won for themselves a precarious independence, a subordinate tradition of small-scale republican government had helped to keep alive the memory of the Roman Republic in which a (select) people had actually exercised political power. As we have seen, however, even in eighteenth-century England monarchy had normally been taken for granted as an indispensable element in a 'mixed' or 'balanced' constitution, and the normal limit of radicalism had been the attempt to make the king responsible via an aristocratic Parliament to a people whose sovereignty was in reserve. The novelty of the American experiment was that it reunited and developed both Roman traditions, calling on the people as constituent sovereign but at the same time as rulers. The new government was emphatically to be a *popular* government. Having gone to war against parliamentary sovereignty in Britain, Americans were determined not to subject themselves to an equivalent sovereign in America. As *The Federalist* insisted, all the different branches of the balanced constitution were to be 'agents' of the people (Hamilton et al. 1886: 292). But although the people were in a sense to be present and active in a government that belonged to them, they were also outside, behind and above their government, still the sovereign in reserve. For the crucial difference between classical republics and the American model lay in 'the total exclusion of the people, in their collective capacity' from the latter (Hamilton et al. 1886: 397). In other words, this was popular government by election, defining the people as voters and thereby bringing them into government while at the same time keeping them at a distance. 'It could be argued [as J. G. A. Pocock observes] both that all government was the people's and that the people had withdrawn from government altogether' (Pocock 1975: 517). The implication was that even where the government was the people's government rather than the king's government, the gap between the government and the sovereign people was still there. This left room for appeals to the people against the people's government; and while these happened routinely during elections, they could never be exhausted by the process of voting. The coexistence of popular government with the authority of the sovereign people in reserve was to set the stage for populism in the sense of movements to 'give government back to the people'.

The Common People and 'Democracy'

Another startling aspect of American politics was that the sovereign 'people' to whom government was to be given back increasingly came to include those previously regarded as the common people (Wood 1992). The levelling implications of the notion of popular sovereignty had been held in check in England by the assumption that landowning gentlemen were the natural representatives of the people as a whole. Although the USA's first generation of leaders were a good deal more meritocratic than their English counterparts, they did not altogether depart from this pattern. But that did not last. The special features of American society that Tocqueville later called 'democracy' (Tocqueville 1862) – the absence of an aristocracy and the extraordinary mobility of the social and economic structure (Boorstin 1988) – made for a conflation of sovereign people and (male, white) common people that emerged in the 1830s in the form of Jacksonian 'democracy'. In his remarkably populist 'Farewell Address' President Andrew Jackson not only insisted on the special character of the USA, 'where the government is emphatically the government of the people . . .'. He also identified 'the people' with 'the planter, the farmer, the mechanic, and the laborer', in effect with the entire free white adult male population, apart from a few financiers and speculators who were conspiring against the people in the 'secret conclave' of the 'organized money power' (Blau 1947: 13–17).

Despite its traditionally unfavourable connotations, the name 'democracy' had already been revived to describe this inclusive popular government.[9] Although this invited Aristotelian worries about majority rule, demagoguery and plundering of property, the unusual structure of American society made possible a new confidence in the common people. The first issue of *The Democratic Review*, published in 1837, declared, 'We have an abiding confidence in the virtue, intelligence, and full capacity for self-government, of the great mass of our people, our industrious, honest, manly, intelligent millions of freemen' (Blau 1947: 22).

So far, then, we can see three of 'the people's' complex strands coming together despite the tensions between them: the people as sovereign, as rulers and as the common people. Two further apparently antithetical strands were added to the American mixture: the people as a specific nation and the people as humanity.

The People as Self-governing Nation

The American Revolution was among other things the first English-speaking *national* revolution, asserting the right not only of the people to rule but of a specific people to rule themselves (Greenfeld 1992). This was particularly striking in view of the assumption previously made on both sides of the Atlantic that the colonists were a branch of the English nation. But it did not take long for the sense of being a distinct people to become established (Bailyn 1967: 20).

Within the British radical discourse of the time, sympathy with American demands for self-determination were linked with parallel claims for a measure of Irish self-government (Butterfield 1949: 92). That link between popular sovereignty, popular government and self-determination for the national people would be passed down to the nineteenth-century tradition of liberal nationalism. The difficulty was to settle the boundaries of the national people. In the USA itself it turned out that only civil war could answer the question of how many 'peoples' there were in the territory. The preamble of the US Constitution had assumed that there was only one, 'We the People of the United States'. But since this people had itself split off from a larger people, the Southern secessionists seemed to be acting on exactly the same principles as their revolutionary forebears when they asserted their own right as a people to rule themselves as they wished, in the interests of their 'peculiar institution' of slavery. When the Civil War was beginning in 1861 Jefferson Davis, President of the Confederate States of America, asserted 'the right of a people to self-government' in the name of 'the people of the Southern States' (Johanssen 1965: 167, 165).

During the lengthy political conflict that had preceded the outbreak of war, 'popular sovereignty' at local level had been proposed as a conciliatory device by Senator Stephen Douglas: a way of solving the dispute between North and South over slavery, and in particular the thorny question whether the institution should be allowed in the new Territories being settled in the American West. Arguing that 'no institution, no law, no constitution, should be forced on an unwilling people contrary to their wishes', Douglas maintained with unconscious irony that 'if the people of a Territory want slavery, they have a right to have it' (Commager 1949: 353). The assumption made here was that the black slaves were in no sense part of 'the people', an exclusion made explicit by the Supreme Court in its 1857 judgement on the Dred Scott case.[10] Few Northern opponents of slavery were prepared to claim explicitly that slaves were or ought to be part of 'the people'; what they were certain of, however, was that slaves were *people*, human beings with natural rights like those claimed in the Declaration of Independence. Earlier generations of republicans had been able to take slavery and other exclusions in their stride, deploying the notion of *populus*/people without being thereby committed to citizenship for all and sundry. But slavery was an intellectual as well as a political problem for Americans because of the universalism to which notions of popular sovereignty had become linked (Pole 1978: 149).

People and 'the People'

The Declaration of Independence claimed self-determination for one specific people in terms of the universal natural rights not only of all 'peoples' but of all people as 'men'. Although the remote political implications of this were not apparent to those who signed the Declaration (Pole 1978: 54–5), there was from the start a strong sense in many quarters in America that the cause of the people there was the cause of humanity everywhere (e.g. Blau 1947: 32). This sense of mission helped to make unacceptable the pragmatic proposal that 'popular sovereignty' could settle the issue of slavery at a local level. It also glossed over the incongruity of a Union army mobilizing to put down a secession that was on the face of it based on the same popular rights as the USA itself. Addressing Congress on 4 July 1861 a few months after Jefferson Davis had taken his secessionist stand on a people's right to self-government, Abraham Lincoln declared in his turn that the Union cause was 'essentially a People's contest', the struggle to maintain a form of government 'whose leading object is to elevate the condition of men'. While asserting that 'the plain people understand, and appreciate this', Lincoln was in effect looking beyond the specific people on either side to people as humanity (Johannsen 1965: 181–2).

One of many reasons why the American Revolution marks a turning-point in the history of the people is that it launched the career of 'the people' as a universalist and progressive cause, with a wide-ranging radical agenda capable of subverting established institutions in the USA itself and around the world. This was not just a matter of asserting popular sovereignty, establishing popular government in place of monarchy and bringing the common people into politics; it was also the cause of oppressed national peoples and the cause of human people everywhere. The effect of the Revolution and its successful outcome was, in other words, to replace the defensive populism of James Burgh and most of his predecessors with the cause of the people as a multifaceted radical project, reverberating from America across Europe and other parts of the world.

The Myth of the Sovereign People in Action

That project took the form not only of ideas but of a powerfully inspiring myth. The story of how the American people had successfully risen against their oppressors and established their own free republic became fixed in the modern political imagination, inspiring imitators far and wide, giving legitimacy to American institutions but also justifying attempts to recall those institutions to their founding principles by giving power back to the people. The mythic dimension of the politics of 'people' will be explored in chapter 6.

5   Popular Sovereignty and Parliamentary Reform in Nineteenth-century Britain

Both the myth and the idea of popular sovereignty were a source of inspiration for many in the nineteenth century. But the significance of America for outsiders was above all that (particularly when glorified by distance) it provided a working model of a polity quite different from the aristocratic monarchy that continued to be the norm (Crook 1965: 2). The American polity was a 'popular government' that included the common people, and it was still there after the French Revolution had disappointed radicals and terrified the propertied classes by sliding into anarchy and dictatorship. Looking across the Atlantic a century after the establishment of the US Constitution, James Bryce remarked that all European visitors scrutinised America as an experiment in democracy, and concluded that although 'the people' really did rule there, the experiment had not borne out the classic critiques of popular power (Bryce 1888: I 1, 8, III 51, 304–21). Consequently, while America was a standing challenge even to the qualified form of aristocratic monarchy that had developed in Britain, American experience did something to moderate the fear of popular government that had for centuries made pragmatic monarchists out of most men of property. Meanwhile, English radicals (including the Chartists who flew the Stars and Stripes at their meetings (Crook 1965: 5)) appealed to the continuing sense of kinship with Americans. When John Bright was campaigning in the mid-nineteenth century for a reform of the suffrage that would 'restore the British constitution in all its fullness . . . to the British people', he drew on successful American experience to ward off fears of the possible effects of extending the suffrage. 'Will any man dare to tell me . . . that the English nation in England is a worse nation than the English nation in America?' (Bright 1868: II, 198, 28).

Large differences in political circumstances between the USA and Britain nevertheless pushed political discourse in different directions, leaving their mark on the meanings of 'the people' on either side of the Atlantic. In contrast to the American experience of a clean break and a new beginning, popular government in Britain evolved gradually in the nineteenth and twentieth centuries within the outward form of aristocratic monarchy, by means of gradual and partial shifts in the interpretation and practice of the constitution (Bagehot 1872: 285). Legally it was Parliament as a whole that was supposed to be sovereign rather than the monarch on one hand or the people on the other. But the successive struggles for parliamentary reform that managed step by step to widen the electorate were invariably waged in the name of popular sovereignty. Once the Reform Act of 1832 had enfranchised the middle classes, the 'people' were increasingly identified in radical rhetoric with the common people or working classes (Stedman Jones 1983: 173). Nevertheless 'the people' was a unifying as well as a divisive notion (Joyce 1991: 11). Although 'working people' were below the crucial social divide between gentlemen and the rest they were still part of the national people, full of national pride in their inherited constitution and surprisingly often prepared to defer to gentlemen as natural representatives of an inclusive people.

Within the politics of nineteenth-century Britain the notion of the people was therefore used in two apparently antithetical ways. One of these was divisive, paving the way for the working-class politics of twentieth-century Britain. The other was unifying, locating class interests and grievances within the struggle by part of the sovereign national people to take their rightful place in a constitution that belonged to them as much as to their betters.

In the early decades of the nineteenth century, during the repressive reaction that followed the French Revolution and the war against Napoleon, embattled radicals in Britain had used the language of 'the people' (in ways that recalled James Burgh) to mean the sovereign in reserve, the entire political community apart from the Court and its hangers-on.[11] But while this inclusive sense of the term was always present in political discourse and its echoes were continually invoked in support of reform, it was the people as common or 'working' people, Cobbett's 'journeymen and labourers' (Thompson 1963: 745), who became increasingly visible in British politics. The aim of radicals from the working people seems to have been above all to get their class recognized as belonging to the national and sovereign people as a whole (Lovett and Collins 1969). To the frustration of some modern left-wing historians, they expressed their demands in the language of 'popular constitutionalism' (Epstein 1994: vii; cf. Joyce 1991) rather than echoing the French Revolutionaries. The radicals of Ashton-under-Lyne who drank a toast to 'the People, the source of all legitimate power' were reaffirming a traditional principle in utterly traditional language – with the crucial difference that the working classes, so very ambiguously included in 'the people' in earlier discourse, were now asserting their right to be heard as the most numerous part of that very people (Epstein 1994: 154).

The People's Charter, at the centre of radical campaigns for parliamentary reform in the 1830s and 1840s, was the most dramatic expression of this claim by the (working) people to take back their inherited constitution from an unrepresentative political class. The phrase, 'we, the people's real representatives' – used in a speech delivered to the Chartist Convention in 1839 – echoes James Burgh's call for a National Association that would represent the sovereign people better than their corrupt Parliament. But whereas Burgh had unselfconsciously assumed that independent men of property were the natural leaders of the people, that 1839 speech was delivered by a master joiner (Epstein 1994: 3). Centuries of English political discourse had seen increasingly confident assertions of the sovereignty of the people that had remained remarkably unconnected (the Levellers apart) with the sense in which the common people were 'the people'. But in the nineteenth century, general acceptance of the once-radical doctrine of ultimate popular sovereignty was sharpened by the American demonstration that this could be turned into a practical and inclusive politics. This helped motivate the long push by British radicals to use the authority of the sovereign and national people as a lever to achieve inclusion of working people. It was in this context that Gladstone was hailed as 'the People's William' (Biagini 2000: 40, 71), and John Bright as 'the Tribune of the People', 'the People's Champion' (Joyce 1994: 142).

This wider political people were becoming harder to ignore, as they were mobilized in increasingly orderly mass demonstrations (Joyce 1994: 202; Biagini 2000: 68) that showed nervous gentlemen both their potential power and their political responsibility. Speaking in the House of Commons in 1859,

John Bright derided upper class fear of 'the people', implying that Tory landowners were afraid because they simply did not know working people: 'The manufacturing, the employing class, does not fear them' (Bright 1868: 99). That fear was in fact neither surprising nor irrational. What many in the propertied classes were afraid of was not just mob violence of the kind that had accompanied the passage of the Great Reform Bill in 1832, but also a rational opposition of interest between rich and poor that would offer opportunity to demagogues (Bagehot 1872: xx, xxvii). If Bright, Gladstone and other gentlemanly radicals did not fear the people, it was because they knew that they could lead the masses.

Despite the much greater visibility of the working people by the mid-nineteenth century, therefore, the British notion of the sovereign people remained hierarchical, a collectivity still led as a matter of course by gentlemen. Reflecting on the differences between Britain and America, Walter Bagehot stressed this 'deference' by the ignorant to the educated classes as the main safeguard against populist plunder of the rich (Bagehot 1872: 262–71; cf. Bryce 1888: III 13). There was a great difference in tone (which was to last at least half-way through the twentieth century – cf. Shils 1956: 48) between American idealization of 'the plain people' as equal to anyone and anything (Hofstadter 1964), and the top-down pathos of 'the people' as viewed even by populists in England.[12]

Be that as it may, in Britain as in America the political language of 'the people' was on balance unifying, turning what might have been experienced as zero-sum economic conflicts into political claims for inclusion in the people as a whole. In so far as it was also divisive, the slice it cut across society did not correspond to Marxist class-divisions. In the 1909 conflict between 'Peers and People' sparked off by Lloyd George's 'People's Budget' (which imposed taxes on landed property to finance social reform) 'the people' in question could (like Andrew Jackson's 'people' eighty years earlier) be plausibly presented as equivalent to the nation (Gilbert 1968: 38–9). As in America, the language of the people was not only a unifying but also a moralising and universalizing force. Patrick Joyce draws attention to what he calls Gladstone's 'moral populism' in which 'the people' widened out to include not only working people of the British nation but also the cause of humanity. During his great Midlothian campaign in 1879 Gladstone told his audience that they themselves, 'a great and free people', held the fate of the empire in their hands. Joyce comments that ' "the people" was slowly expanding until it became all people. The people could speak for all people . . .' – all humanity (Joyce 1994: 206). One side-effect of British imperialism and colonialism was indeed to spread the discourse of 'people' far and wide, handing conceptual and rhetorical tools to opponents of empire.

6   Popular Government and the People

In Britain by the end of the nineteenth century, then, the political people was becoming more and more inclusive – extending downwards into the working class, outwards to humanity and even sideways to women,[13] and yet 'the people' were still somehow *special*, united in moral privilege. That morally special people were still trying to take back their sovereign power, first by struggling for the vote and then in the long campaign by the Labour Party to capture the state for the (working) people. To that extent people and power were still distinguished from one another and would continue to be so until the Second World War.

The USA in the late nineteenth century saw a different kind of populism, born not so much of the struggle for popular inclusion as of disappointment with its results. Popular government in practice had not, after all, turned out to be a recipe for virtue and progress. The American Republic had reunited the two strands of the Roman legacy, with ambiguous implications. On the one hand it had established popular government, giving the people the opportunity to oversee what was done in their name; at the same time, however, it had left the sovereign and constituent people their ultimate authority in reserve. Since the government was elected by the people, up to a point its actions were their actions, but *only* up to a point. In normal circumstances the gap between people and people's government could be closed at election time by turning the rascals out, but sometimes it loomed so wide that it prompted a more radical mobilization against parties and politicians in general. In the words of the 1892 Omaha Platform of the

People's Party, Populists saw their movement as a crusade 'to restore the government of the Republic to the hands of "the plain people" with whose class it originated' (Pollack 1967: 59) in the expectation that such a restoration would solve their problems and bring about a new dawn.

Americans were the first in modern times to achieve popular government, and therefore the first to experience this disillusionment, this sense that the people's government had somehow escaped from the control of the people. There have been many subsequent cases and many calls for institutional fixes to give government back to the people, notably through the use of referendums and initiatives. But the conundrum of the people in reserve, with their special moral status, is that *any* such arrangement is open to challenge: none can be decisively said to capture the voice of the people. One response to the disappointments of democracy is to remain true to the populist project and to keep looking for that elusive people. Another response, altogether more disenchanted, takes the view that government by the people is actually nothing more than government by *people* – by human beings – and that inflated expectations are quite inappropriate.

The glamour and pathos of the people throughout its history have depended on contrasts: the sovereign people contrasted with the sovereign monarch, the common people with the privileged classes, the national people with foreigners. Popular government, whether Roman or American, was similarly contrasted with its opposite, carrying the fascination of being a special kind of government in a world where kingship or tyranny was the norm, or (in the American case) the model that all mankind must eventually copy. In the twenty-first century such contrasts are harder to find. Ruling kings have virtually disappeared, and although plenty of tyrants survive, they are shabby and lack much claim to legitimacy. In Anglophone countries the 'common people' have ceased to be a distinct class and have disappeared into 'ordinary people'; it is even claimed by some that distinct national peoples are losing their sharp edges in a globalized world of people-as-human-beings. In a sense what has happened could be seen as the triumph of the politics of 'people', but in becoming omnipresent it has lost as much as it has gained. As a natural constituency for progressive causes 'the people' have turned out to be no more reliable than the proletariat; self-determination by a national people is not, it seems, a recipe for getting rid of oppression; above all, government of the people by the people is just a set of contingent and complex arrangements for the rule of some human beings by others.

A key development of the twentieth century, in other words, was the fading of 'the people' into the population, an ad-hoc collection of individual human beings inside the contingent boundaries of a state. But this does not mean that we can wave goodbye to the people as an immortal sovereign body, nor as a specially chosen nation, nor as a common people with common interests, nor as the bearers of a progressive crusade against oppression. Although the neutral sense of 'people' is now commonplace, modern politics continues to be haunted by inherited myths and discourses and their associated claims and dilemmas. In particular, it is more than ever assumed that the only source of legitimate political authority is the consent of the people.

Conclusion

I have tried in this chapter to provide a brief sketch of the ways in which the notion and language of 'the people' have been used, adapted and extended in the course of past political struggles, especially within the Anglophone politics of the last few centuries but also within the older traditions on which those struggles drew. While the survey underlines the significance of 'the people' as ultimate political authority, it also illustrates the range of meanings and internal tensions that give the notion both its rhetorical usefulness and its conceptual obscurity. What we have inherited is a cluster of ideas and discourses that are indispensable but deeply problematic. In pursuit of greater clarity, the rest of the book will explore two sets of politically significant ambiguities. The first set concerns the people's boundaries, external and internal; the second the people's sovereign authority, in action and in myth. While the problems to be addressed arise from current politics and must be addressed in contemporary terms, persistent echoes of older struggles should perhaps warn us that easy solutions are not likely to be ready to hand.

3

Ourselves and Others: People, Nation and Humanity

all public powers . . . come from the people, that is to say, the nation.

Emmanuel Sieyès in Hont 1994

When the French revolutionaries issued their 'Declaration of the Rights of Man and of the Citizen' in 1789, they challenged absolute monarchy by attributing sovereignty to 'the nation'. This interpretation of the principle of popular sovereignty offended Robespierre and other radicals, who took the view that it was too restrictive, since nations should be seen only as local branches of the true sovereign people, the whole human race (Hont 1994: 207–09). In the abstract Robespierre's view may seem reasonable; if the people is indeed the source of political authority, shouldn't it include all people and be coextensive with humanity? But in ordinary political discourse it is always *a* people to whom sovereignty is attributed or whose consent is required for legitimacy; a people somehow marked off from people in general. So what should we understand by 'a people' for political purposes? Is it equivalent to a nation or to an ethnic group? Can a people be a political community of a different kind, cross-cutting or transcending national or ethnic ties? And whatever the nature of their communal bonds, how can the rights of bounded, exclusive peoples be reconciled with the claims of people as human beings in general? These questions have often been overlooked within a political discourse that tends to equate 'peoples' with the populations of existing states. But contemporary political problems are making them harder to ignore. Boundaries are being put in question both by the secessionist claims of self-styled 'peoples' and by transnational projects like the European Union. At the same time, accelerating migration underlines the continuing importance of boundaries between 'our people' (who are the possessors of democratic rights and ultimate source of political authority) and other people around the world who want to join them.

These are the themes of the present chapter. Section 1 considers the link between 'people' and 'nation'. Although the two are often treated as equivalent, there are some grounds within the republican tradition of political thought for conceiving of 'a people' as a political community that is neither a nation nor an ethnic group. Section 2 will pursue this theme by considering projects for the building of transnational peoples, in particular the belief that a single European people can be made to form the basis of a fully democratic European Union. Even if that extension of popular solidarity were achieved, however, it would not alter the fact that any specific people has boundaries and that members of a democratic people enjoy rights and powers denied to people in general. Section 3 looks at the tensions between democratic commitments to 'our people' and those to people as such. One way of easing democratic consciences has been to regard our own people as in some sense a 'chosen people', with a mission to all people and corresponding privileges. That comfortable solution looks less appealing in the harsh light cast on boundaries by the contemporary politics of migration, which makes it harder both to ignore and to resolve the tensions within the politics of peoplehood.

1 People and Nation

> All peoples have the right of self-determination. By virtue of
> that right they freely determine their political status and freely
> pursue their economic, social and cultural development.
>   T. D. Musgrave, *Self-determination and National Minorities*

This momentous declaration appears as Article 1 of each of the two International Human Rights Covenants that were adopted by the United Nations in 1966 and came into force ten years later. Given general acceptance of the principle of popular sovereignty it may seem merely a statement of the obvious. The problem is, what is a 'people'? How are the collectivities that have the right of self-determination to be identified? The international agreements that incorporated the article did not answer this question, leaving jurists frustrated by the difficulties of applying the principle to specific political disputes (Musgrave 1997: 148–79; cf. Cassese 1995). In some cases, referendums can allow the population to identify themselves as members of one or several peoples. But it often happens in territorial disputes that there is no democratic way of demarcating a 'people'. The question cannot simply be put to the people themselves, because there is no agreement on the boundaries of the constituency and therefore on which people are entitled to vote (Whelan 1983).

Within the post-war international context in which it was adopted, the declaration's purpose was to hasten decolonization by demanding self-rule for territories that had been carved out in the course of empire-building with scant regard for the boundaries of existing communities. 'People' in this context did not imply the existence of collective consciousness or solidarity; in the eyes of those who adopted the declaration, a 'people' was simply the population who happened to find themselves within a given set of territorial boundaries, and 'nation-building' was supposed to follow independence, not precede it. This lack of any specific content for 'a people' was politically expedient at the time and momentous in retrospect, but it was untypical. Within political and theoretical discourse both before and since the declaration, the 'peoples' to whom rights to self-determination have been attributed have usually been seen either as nations, or else as ethnic groups sharing an inherited culture, such as indigenous peoples. Despite the influence of this ethno-national way of thinking, however, a political people can in principle be conceived in another way. Within the western political tradition, classical republicans long preserved the notion of a *populus* that was the political community of a *city*, understood as an artefact that was neither nation nor tribe. Drawing on certain republican themes, some contemporary political thinkers seek to distinguish 'people' from 'nation' in order to free democratic accountability and popular consent from what seem to them to be unacceptable ethnic associations – a project that will be assessed in section 2. The main concern of the present section is to examine the close conceptual and practical connection between political 'people' and (more or less ethnic) 'nation', and for that some conceptual ground-clearing is required.

Nationhood is notoriously difficult to define, and is almost as contentious a matter in theory as it is in practice. Those controversies cannot be reviewed here; however, I have argued elsewhere that nationhood is elusive because it is essentially a mediating phenomenon, a (variable) blend of the ethnic and the political that holds together nature and artifice, past and present, fate and will. A nation is not equivalent to an ethnic group, but the common equation of the national with the ethnic is not surprising because a nation does to some extent need to *feel* ethnic; to be a community that is experienced as possessing depths of history, culture and kinship at the same time as being a political people (Canovan 1996). This is not to say that every political people must necessarily be a nation; non-national peoples have existed in the past (at least in city-states) and may conceivably be possible in the future. But it is certainly the norm in modern politics for a political people that can plausibly be regarded as a subject of self-determination to be a nation, and it can be argued that there is a close connection between nation-hood and the exercise of popular sovereignty, including the possibility of representative government and liberal democracy (Canovan 2002b). This point was indeed made in typically pragmatic style by John Stuart Mill in his *Considerations on Representative Government*, published in 1861. Mill pointed out that the 'common sympathies' of fellow-nationals eased political co-operation among them, whereas lack of 'fellow-feeling' and common culture was bound to inhibit the forma-tion of public opinion. Not only was there a prima facie case for a national government 'where the sentiment of nationality exists in any force', but (Mill observed) 'this is merely saying that the question of government ought to be decided by the governed' (Mill 1962: 309). In other words, popular sovereignty and national self-determination are intertwined.

The precise nature of that connection can be analysed in different ways. A striking account of the mutual reinforcement provided for one another by people and nation has been given by Bernard Yack. He maintains that 'the people' is an abstract image of political community that needs the historic solidarity of the nation to give it substance: 'the nation provides precisely what is lacking in the concept of the people: a sense of where to look for the prepolitical basis of political community'. For whereas (in his view) the people presents a timeless image of community existing across territorial *space*, the nation supplies 'an image of community *over time*. What binds us into national communities is our image of a shared heritage that is passed, in modified form, from one generation to another.' The effect of this symbiosis has been 'to nationalize political loyalties and politicize national loyalties'. Yack concludes that nationalism is closely linked with democracy, much more closely than its critics suppose (Yack 2001: 524, 520, 523, 530).

Yack's argument rests upon an understanding of the sovereign people as a purely abstract collectivity, an understanding that does not (in my view) allow enough space for the complexities of the notion. These will be examined at length in chapter 5, where I shall argue that the sovereign people cannot be satisfactorily analysed simply as an abstraction, since individual people can in principle give it concrete presence by mobilizing collectively for action. But because such collective action is occasional, partial and ephemeral, Yack's analysis of the people's relation to time and history remains relevant whether or not we can accept his account as a whole. Yack's abstract people needs nationhood to give it a historic location because it is outside history and 'exists in a kind of eternal present' (Yack 2001: 521). The concrete, mobilized people we occasionally encountered in the last chapter is certainly not eternally present; on the contrary, it is more usually absent. But it is outside time in the sense that it has no continuous history, and that each appearance of a mobilized people is a fresh start. In a sense it is the mobilization itself, the engagement of individual people in collective action, that constitutes a people where none existed before, and may in due course give rise to a nation.[1] There can be no doubt, however, that a previous history as a national people is a great help to such mobilization, nor that nations are good at preserving and perpetuating these fleeting moments of popular action. As Yack says, it is of the essence of nations to exist in time and to pass collective memories, myths and symbols from one generation to another. When the recollection of some great moment of popular mobilization is enshrined in national memory, this is bound to make it easier to mobilize individuals as a people in the future. The fleeting collective power generated by action in concert can in this way be stored as if in a battery, ready to power future action[2] (Canovan 1996: 72–4; cf. Smith 2003).

The net effect of these arguments is to suggest that the politics of popular sovereignty is likely to be most powerful where *the* people can act as *a* people because they form a nation. There is certainly a strong historic link between assertions of popular sovereignty and of national self-determination in struggles for 'liberation'. Fused in the anti-Communist revolutions of 1989 in Eastern Europe, the two had already been linked in most of the revolutions that ended dynastic empires in Europe after the First World War, in the attempted national/liberal revolutions of 1848 and in the French Revolution itself. The connection is symbolized by the debate in the revolutionary National Assembly in 1789 in which it was decided that the contemporary French equivalent of *populus*, the source of sovereignty, was '*la nation*' (Hont 1994: 194).[3] Still further back in history, the revolutionary assertion of popular sovereignty in seventeenth-century England was closely tied to the long-standing English sense of belonging to a national people with a uniquely free political heritage.

Unconscious reliance on national peoplehood has long been embedded in Anglophone political culture, with effects on political theory (Canovan 1996) and political practice. Where the issue of self-determination is concerned it has sometimes led to dangerously naive politics, as defenders of self-determination took for granted that the individual people living in a given territory would add up to *a* people able to determine their own political future. In the absence of nationhood this has often proved illusory. Note, however, that the crucial factor may be the absence of nationhood rather than the presence of ethnic diversity. A nation is not an ethnic group, even though it is always conceived to a greater or lesser extent in terms of kinship and inheritance. Nations vary a great deal, and while the much-abused distinction between 'ethnic' and 'civic' nations is unhelpfully crude, it is certainly true that the proportion of ethnic to civic elements varies in different cases; Irish nationhood is more ethnic than British nationhood, for example, and German than French. The most civic and least ethnic of all, though still with ethnic elements (Yack 1996) is of course American nationhood, in which a population drawn from remarkably diverse ethnic and national origins is united in a collectivity of formidable solidarity. Although the English nationhood shared by most free residents at the time of the Revolution no doubt helped in holding the colonies together (and was stressed by Federalists for this purpose – Hamilton et al. 1886: 9) – the formation of a separate American national identity followed rather than preceded mobilization as a political *people*, a people, moreover, that was self-consciously making a fresh start in a new Republic. The USA's remarkable capacity to integrate diverse ethnic groups into the nation owes a good deal to the priority given to peoplehood in a sense that perhaps has more in common with the Roman *populus* than with the ethnic *Volk* of nineteenth-century Romanticism.

When seen from a distance, American experience can make national peoplehood in a multi-ethnic society look deceptively easy. A similar ideal has been articulated in a less optimistic tone by the French political theorist Dominique Schnapper. Against a background of consumerist individualism and rising ethnic consciousness inside the state, and weakening national sovereignty without, she sets out to defend the French Republican ideal of the nation as a 'community of citizens'. For Schnapper, a nation is a distinctively *political* community defined by a particular historic political project. The community is formed by a deliberate process of education (repeated in each generation) that lifts individuals above the limitations of their personal and ethnic identities into the universality of a shared political life as equal citizens. Even a deliberately constructed nation of this kind still needs, as Schnapper admits, to draw upon quasi-natural communal feelings and a quasi-ethnic heritage of history and language. Central to the book, however, is a conception of the political community as a deliberate achievement and current project rather than as an organic growth (Schnapper 1994). Despite celebrating this 'community of citizens' Schnapper fears that its days are numbered. Unable to exercise external sovereignty in a globalized world, its citizens distracted from political life by economic preoccupations on the one hand and inter-ethnic tensions on the other, the republican nation may be on the way out. The book's tone is as classically republican as its main theme, echoing the pessimism of a tradition that saw polities as human constructions and therefore doomed to eventual ruin; in that vein, Rousseau included in his portrait of the ideal polity an account of the state's inevitable decline, exclaiming, 'If Sparta and Rome perished, what state can hope to last forever?' (Rousseau 1987: 194). But Schnapper's anxieties, like her understanding of nationhood, are perhaps best understood within the specific context of French history and French prospects in a world that is increasingly Anglophone and increasingly dominated by the United States. Some political thinkers outside that context share similar republican commitments but look with a different eye on nations and their possible eclipse. For some, a future in which nation-states lose their *raison d'être* seems to offer an opportunity for non-national peoples to come into their own, and perhaps even for the formation of a people that will comprehend *all* people. In some ways these proposals for a non-national politics of peoplehood merely take to their logical conclusion themes already present in the more 'Roman' versions of nationhood, such as Schnapper's. But there is a crucial difference. It is of the essence of nationhood (as even Schnapper admits) to make political community seem natural and given; 'to turn chance into destiny', in Benedict Anderson's words (Anderson 1983: 19). This is of course an illusion; despite the huge and undiminished emotional and political force of that myth of national destiny, it can scarcely be denied that all political peoples – even national peoples – have been constituted through political action and that their boundaries are contingent. But once that contingency is recognized, the construction of political peoples that cross-cut or transcend national boundaries may seem possible, at any rate to political thinkers willing to discount the power of national myths. The notion of building such a non-national people is the focus of section 2.

2   People-building

> He who dares to undertake the establishment of a people should
> feel that he is, so to speak, in a position to change human
> nature, to transform each individual (who by himself is a perfect
> and solitary whole) into a part of a larger whole from which
> this individual receives, in a sense, his life and his being.
>
> Rousseau, 'On the Social Contract'

Since the spread of Romantic nationalism in the nineteenth
century 'a people' has had *völkisch* associations, suggesting a
rural people with a distinctive language and customs, closer to
nature than city-dwellers. Until relatively recently this rural
connection was reinforced by use of 'the people' to refer to a
'common people' composed largely of peasants and farm
workers. As we have already seen, however, the notion of a
distinct political people also belongs within the older and
emphatically urban ideal of the *populus* of a city-republic, an
ideal that was still alive when the French Revolution broke out
in 1789, though it was soon to be eclipsed by the rise of
Romanticism.

In a fascinating study in intellectual history, Martin Thom
has identified a change in European political imagery that took
place about 1800, 'the yielding of a world of cities to a world of
nations' (Thom 1995: 2). The classical republican ideal of the
city-state, still cherished by Rousseau, was abruptly displaced
by a new enthusiasm for the 'tribe', the barbarian ancestors to
which nineteenth-century Romantic nationalists looked for the
ethnic origins of their nations. Thom shows that this change of
focus had wide-ranging implications. Where 'peoples' are concerned, the vital difference was a contrast between nature and
artifice. Romantic nationalists liked to think that their peoples
were part of the order of nature, growing to maturity in an
organic process of historical development, whereas classical
republicans had always taken the view that a people of citizens
was no more of a natural growth than the city they inhabited.
Cities needed to be built, and so (according to republican traditions) did peoples, usually by some heroic founder or lawgiver
like Lycurgus of Sparta (Rousseau 1987: 162–6; Thom 1995:
69–85). In the republican imagination the people is a product of
political will. Because the city is artificial, its original inhabitants

must have been drawn out of their natural habitat and loyalties before being welded into a people. Later generations may inherit citizenship and show a Roman piety to their ancestors, but their piety and patriotism cannot be taken for granted and must be deliberately cultivated.

Does the contrast between 'Roman' and 'Romantic' habits of thought provide intellectual resources to help modern political thinkers develop non-national ways of thinking about peoples? Some modern critics of nationalism believe that by recovering features of the classical republican tradition we can reinterpret what it is to be a people in ways that detach it entirely from ethnic Romanticism. Before we explore these reinterpretations, let us pause for a moment to consider the point of this move. If nationhood has for good reasons been closely associated with popular sovereignty and democracy, why might one want to detach 'people' from nation? One reason is no doubt the sense in some quarters that the nation-state has had its day and cannot cope with globalization. But the revulsion against nations and nationalism shared by many political thinkers goes deeper than that, and stems from two factors, negative and positive. The negative aspect is the memory of Nazism and the fear that because of their ethnic elements all nations are tarred with the same brush. Complementing this negative reaction is the positive attraction of a universalist liberalism that transcends and trumps national boundaries and loyalties (Nussbaum et al. 1996). Combining the two, one might say schematically that anti-nationalists seek an understanding of 'people' (as opposed to 'nation') that will be compatible with the following commitments:

1 A peaceful acceptance of differences in place of militarism and genocide.
2 Shared humanity and equal human rights for all people in place of the exclusive claims of a superior *Volk*.
3 Membership based on political will and individual choice, not determined by genetic make-up.

Unfortunately for cosmopolitan liberals, finding an understanding of what it is to be a people that satisfies all these conditions is exceedingly difficult. The problem cannot be solved simply by rejecting the Romantic *Volk* in favour of the Roman *populus*. The latter fails on point (1) because the classical republican patriotism that was its bond was decidedly militaristic, with a ruthlessness that was savoured by Machiavelli (Machiavelli 1970). As for (2), membership of a classical republican people was a proud and jealously guarded privilege, and those who enjoyed it were not in the least inclined to equate their fellow-citizens with people in general. Faithfully echoing this aspect of the tradition, Rousseau maintained that contempt and indifference toward those outside the political community was the price of solidarity inside it. 'Every patriot hates foreigners. They are only men, and nothing to him' (Rousseau 1911: 7). On these first two points, in other words, the people of classical republicanism is no more congenial to modern liberalism than its Romantic counterpart. Point (3), however, contrasting biological determinism with political will, does offer more scope to the modern liberal. It is true that classical traditions are not entirely satisfactory even in this respect. Rome's wide expansion of citizenship did not amount to liberal universalism, while the familial imagery of Roman political culture and the stress on piety toward the people's ancestors seem suspiciously tribal. But despite the problems encountered by those who want to fend off nationalism by reviving the tradition of a people bound together by patriotism (Viroli 1995; Canovan 2000) there really is one important difference between Romantic and Roman conceptions of what it is to be a people, and that is the contrast between nature and artifice: between conceiving of a people as an organic growth or as the outcome of political will.

I shall argue later that this influential contrast is seriously misleading because it leaves out a third and more plausible account. All the same, it is easy to see the attraction of the republican stress on political will, for it seems to offer the ultimate possibility of overcoming the dissonance between bounded 'peoples' on the one hand and people in general on the other. If the political peoples that democracy requires are in no sense natural communities, if their cohesion and boundaries are products of political will, might it not then be possible (if only in the very long run) to build a 'people' that would incorporate *all* people? Contemporary liberal thought is haunted by this vision of the people as a universal political project, with the result that nationalism even in its milder

versions is condemned for sanctifying divisions within humanity that ought to be regarded as temporary. Reviving memories
of forgotten city-republics may from that point of view seem
worthwhile simply because they show that political peoples do
not have to be nations. Before the era of nation-states there
were already such peoples in existence, if mostly on a small
scale. It may be, therefore, that the coincidence of people and
nation has been a temporary phase in political development,
one that is now coming to its end. Globalization is making
inroads on the sovereignty of most national peoples, while the
migration it encourages makes them ever less homogeneous.
Might there be both a need and an opportunity to exercise
political will and to build polities and peoples that transcend
nations and reach out to humanity? The most favoured site for
this project is the ever-expanding European Union.

People-building in the European Union

'Nation-building' is a project that has been much talked
about (if less often accomplished); 'people-building', by contrast, is an unfamiliar notion.[4] And yet it could be argued
that the latter ought to be the more plausible project of the
two because of the time-dimension of nationhood. Nations,
however republican in style, need historical depth to confer the
illusion of naturalness that is part of their stock in trade. Even
if (as is usually the case) the nation's 'history' includes a good
deal of myth, it takes a few generations to give the stories an
authentic veneer of antiquity. The European Union contains
some of the most deeply rooted nations in existence, making
implausible the idea of building a single European nation to
displace them in the affections of EU citizens. But if a single
European nation is a forlorn hope, might there not in the
forseeable future be the possibility of a European *people*: a
political people on a transnational scale, recalling the Roman
populus that spanned an empire? It is notorious that no such
European people exists as yet; jurists, politicians and theorists
worry that EU institutions lack legitimacy because of the
absence of a single sovereign people that could authorize them.
When the German Federal Constitutional Court declared in
1993 that there was no European *demos*, there was controversy

about what sort of *demos* a polity might need, but the fact of the matter was scarcely in dispute (Weiler 1995; Grimm 1995; Hayward 1995). Believers in the project of 'ever-closer union' within the EU agree that a European people is needed; but how might such a people be built?

The answers suggested by the classical republican tradition are not encouraging. The peoples of classical polities shared face-to-face participation in a common project and were built through personal contacts, permanent mobilization against outsiders, rituals of solidarity and the deliberate inculcation of patriotism (Oldfield 1990; Rahe 1992). Rousseau insisted on the need for a 'civil religion' even in the confined bounds of a city-state; his Jacobin followers started as enemies of the nation-state, but turned into rabid French nationalists as they discovered the mobilizing potential of the nation (Hont 1994). None of this can give much comfort to Europhiles. Many of them would, however, choose not to look back into history for a model but to gaze across the Atlantic to the USA. At first sight the American example is more encouraging, appearing to show that a people on a vast scale can be built out of a heterogeneous collection of diverse materials. Why should not veneration of a Constitution, civic education and the cult of the flag be able to bind citizens together as effectively in Europe as in the USA?

To suggest the parallel is also to expose its implausibility. The problem is not only that the national loyalties already present inside the EU get in the way; even if that hurdle were lower, no civil religion can be inculcated into the young (especially in circumstances of free expression) unless there is a substantial cadre of true believers who have faith in the mission of the polity and enthusiasm to preach the Word. The American people has been sustained from the start by the widely-shared belief that it is a special, chosen people engaged in a project that has significance for all humanity. In section 3 we will need to consider the importance of chosen peoplehood in bridging the gap between bounded, exclusive peoplehood on the one hand and people as humanity on the other. But the contrast in civic faith between the USA and the European Union is striking. The original architects of what became the EU were indeed inspired by the vision of a new community, but this was always the faith of a tiny elite, never engaging the wider population and posing little threat to national loyalties. Twenty-first century Europeans, embarrassed by the persistence of the American sense of mission, seem unlikely to be converted to a parallel faith, unless perhaps some catastrophic crisis should mobilize the whole population of the EU against a common threat from outside. And even the perception of an external threat might not produce the desired European solidarity. The contrast with the USA is only underlined by the revitalization of popular American patriotism following 11 September 2001, for the threat of Islamist fundamentalism that has mobilized America has tended only to divide Europe. It is hard to see what sort of common 'story of peoplehood' EU members could embrace (Smith 2003).

It may be a mistake, however, to think of people-building within the European Union in terms of civic faith or shared stories. Is it not possible that a single European people can be formed by less obtrusive means, simply through common experience of political engagement and deliberation? The most celebrated advocate of this project, Jürgen Habermas, has repeatedly dismissed the objection that no European 'people' exists by calling for the creation of an EU-wide public sphere within which political discourse could be carried on and shared across Europe. Immersion in this discourse would itself give rise to European solidarity, and to a shared 'constitutional patriotism' different both from nationalism and from the tight, exclusive patriotism of the classical republican tradition.

'Constitutional patriotism' will come up for discussion when we consider the tension between bounded peoples and people as humanity. First, though, let us look more closely at Habermas's hopes for the building of a European people through the mediation of a European public sphere. The first point to be made about this is a negative one: not only is there (so far) no European people; neither is there any common European public sphere. The obstacles were clearly set out in a 1995 article by Dieter Grimm to which Habermas himself responded. Grimm pointed out that popular politics in the EU is conducted at the national level, not by means of Europe-wide parties, movements or campaigns. Any developments of that sort would need a 'Europeanised communications system', that is to say 'newspapers and periodicals, radio and television programmes, offered and demanded on a European market and thus creating a nation-transcending communicative context. But such a market would presuppose a public with language skills enabling it to utilize European media' (Grimm 1995: 294–5). Lack of a common language is, in other words, one of the biggest obstacles to the formation of a European people.

Habermas's response to this article was interesting. He did not dispute Grimm's diagnosis of the current situation but he refused to accept the argument that we must give up further efforts to build a single European polity and fall back on the nation-state. Rejecting the notion that a people needs to exist before a democratic polity can function, he argued that collective identity develops through the workings of the democratic process itself. This process does indeed demand the creation of 'a European-wide, integrated public sphere' including political parties, social movements and interest groups that operate across the EU, but Habermas evidently regards the creation of all these conditions as a matter of political will. He is not deterred even by the enormous hurdle of linguistic diversity, in view of the widespread use of English as a second language and the potential for linguistic education (Habermas 1995: 307). In the end, his position is that a reluctant population can be turned into a European people by leadership, through 'the political will of competent actors' (Habermas 2001: 24).

This stress on top-down political will recalls the superhuman legislators of the classical republican tradition, who created peoples by making use of individual people who were raw material rather than agents in the process. In defence of this Lycurgan – or Napoleonic – aspiration, Habermas argues that European national solidarities were themselves artificially constructed in the nineteenth century by measures that included state education and mass conscription (Habermas 1999: 57–8; 2001: 16). Why, then, should not popular solidarity be deliberately stretched across the European Union, as a step on the way (ultimately) to citizenship of the world (Habermas 1996a)? This project raises two important and problematic questions about peoplehood:

1 Even if political peoples are not natural entities, does it follow that they are artificial in the sense that they can be made to order? May they not instead be the contingent outcomes of uncontrollable mobilization?

2 The borders of any people are certainly contingent and
    may be expandable, but they remain borders; can they ever
    stretch to include all people?

On the first point, Habermas's project for the deliberate
building of a European people draws on the familiar opposition
between nature and artifice that we encountered in contrasting
'Romantic' and 'Roman' views of how peoples come to exist.
Discussion in these terms implies that only two alternatives
are available: either a people is a natural, organic growth,
a Romantic *Volk*, or else it is an artificial political construction deliberately brought into existence by a leader or elite in
control of the process. As I suggested earlier, this contrast leaves
out a third and more plausible possibility. A people may not
be a natural, organic growth but it may not be a deliberate, artificial construction either. Instead, it may be the contingent
outcome of intersecting actions by a multitude of political
actors, none of them in a position to foresee or control the
result. Peoples may come into existence not by being built but
by being mobilized – and mobilization, which sets people in
motion, is a much more open-ended business than 'building'.
    This third account seems better than either of the others at
describing the emergence in England and in America of political peoples that were neither natural nor designed, but were
the result of individuals acting together on particular occasions
in response to particular crises. Once an American people
existed, it was indeed perpetuated by deliberate socializa-
tion of immigrants, the cult of the flag and so on, but this was
secondary to the popular mobilization that formed a people
in the first place. The paradox of Habermas's theory (echoing
the paradox of the legislator that haunts classical republicanism) is that it is hard to see how such a top-down process
could deliver a *democratic* people or indeed be carried out by
democratic methods. Like the classical republican tradition,
Habermas seems to be making the mistake (identified by
Hannah Arendt) of confusing political action with *making*
things. 'Making' or 'building' implies an artificer in control of
inert material, whereas politics is a plural and intractable affair
of many political actors reacting to one another's initiatives, in
ways that vastly complicate the path from project to result. On
the occasions when many individuals manage to act together

they can generate unexpected levels of collective power, as popular mobilizations have repeatedly shown. In many cases, strong leadership is indeed a crucial ingredient. But the plural capacity for action that lies at the root of politics continually frustrates attempts to predict and control the outcome of projects, including projects for 'people-building' (Arendt 1998).

Rejecting Romantic notions that a people is a natural growth does not therefore entitle us to suppose that it can be made to order. All it implies is that the existence of a people is contingent. Deliberate attempts to bring it into existence may sometimes help, but they may have no effect or may even (like some ill-fated attempts at 'nation-building') set off resistance to the point of being counter-productive. In any case, historical experience of the circumstances in which popular mobilization has commonly happened – in opposition to some enemy – suggests that any future European people may not be the liberal, tolerant, outward-looking kind of people that Habermas would like. His problem is that although he would like to see enough European popular solidarity to transcend national feeling, this must be solidarity of a very special kind, because it must form a step on the way to universal peoplehood. The difficulties of this ambivalent project are evident in Habermas's celebrated notion of 'constitutional patriotism' in which the object of the patriot's devotion is not 'my country, right or wrong' but the set of liberal democratic principles enshrined in the country's constitution. This substitute for national loyalty is intended to be at one and the same time a bond of loyalty to one's own particular polity and a commitment to universal liberal principles transcending all boundaries (Habermas 1996a).

The notion of 'constitutional patriotism' has been much criticized (e.g. Canovan 2000) and it is easy to point out that in his project for a single European people Habermas seems to want to have things both ways: to have the popular consciousness and solidarity that a democracy needs if the polity is to be strong and the government accountable, while at the same time avoiding particularism and closure, and reaching out on the wings of universal liberal principles to touch all people everywhere. We need to acknowledge, however, that this inconsistency is a response to genuine dilemmas that plague liberal democracy both in theory and in practice.

Habermas, Andrew Linklater and others are right to draw attention to the moral impetus within liberalism that has led to the widening and deepening of citizenship inside liberal states, and to point out that this progressive inclusion of previously excluded groups calls into question the fundamental distinction between insiders and outsiders (Linklater 1998, 1999). The formation of a European people would not overcome this dilemma of exclusion, just move it to a different location.

The fundamental dilemma lies in the very notion of the sovereign people. As a collectivity, the people must have edges, and yet any such boundaries can only be contingent; why, therefore, should peoplehood stop at this particular set of frontiers, especially when people are queueing up to join? In rejecting Romantic notions of 'natural' peoplehood, liberals have in a sense sharpened the dilemmas of inclusion and exclusion. The more we recognize that the boundaries of any particular people are accidental, the harder it becomes to justify the exclusion of specific individual people from membership. This theoretical clash between the universal and the particular is made flesh in the persons of the immigrants and asylum-seekers who flock into the rich liberal democracies of the West. Are we obliged to conclude, then, that the concept of the people is detachable not only from nationhood but from any boundaries at all, and that it points to universal inclusion in a people of *all* people? The political and ethical dilemmas involved here are deep and dangerous. The next section will look first at a way of trying to bridge the gap between peoples and people that has often tempted western democrats, and then at the issue that most glaringly highlights the tensions in the politics of peoplehood: migration across borders.

3   Peoples and People

A Mission to All People

The politics of peoplehood has often managed to combine two potentially divergent themes: local mobilization of a particular people, and universal solidarity with people in general. One way of doing this is to credit others with the rights we are claiming for ourselves, and call on them to follow our example. Thus Tom Paine defended the people's sovereignty against kingship first in America, then in France and Britain, urging all specific peoples to follow suit and assert their rights (Paine 1989). It often happens, however, that the relation between our people and people in general is more complicated than this. Because it is a movement on behalf of all people everywhere, a universalist politics of the people may be explicitly conceived as crossing and overriding differences between peoples. Movements of this kind (such as many versions of international socialism) tend in principle to oppose claims on behalf of particular peoples. But because the vanguard of such a movement must be located in some particular place, this accidental localization of the universal cause can shade imperceptibly into a universalization of the local, with the result that one specific people sees itself as the carrier of a universal message and the representative of all humanity (cf. Canovan 1998). The French Revolution dramatically illustrated this identification between a specific people and a universal mission. Having asserted the sovereignty of people against kings, the revolutionaries issued a general offer to aid other peoples in rebellion and embarked on a crusade to liberate the people of Europe. In the course of this triumphant crusade, however, the interests of the international people's revolution became identified with the interests of the specific people evidently chosen by destiny to lead that Revolution – the French. All those in 'liberated' countries who sided with the international people's cause were dubbed 'patriots'; an ambiguous title, at first glance a precursor of Habermas's 'constitutional patriotism' but in practice often applied to those regarded as French agents and traitors to their own people. As for the English people (the traditional enemies of the French), in Robespierre's eyes they became arch-traitors to the universal cause. In a debate at the Jacobin Club in 1794 he dismissed any notion that the target of the war was England's government rather than its people, exclaiming to applause from the audience, 'As a Frenchman, as a representative of the people, I declare that I hate the English people' (Hont 1994: 225).

This paradoxical union of universal commitments with particular dominance was striking because of the speed with which it evolved and the mobilizing power of both its clashing elements; the causes of universal revolution on the one hand and of French nationalism on the other. But the basic pattern of thought was familiar enough. The notion of a particular chosen people with a mission to dominate and enlighten the world was present in Roman patriotic literature and in the Old Testament, and inspired many imitators. In the sixteenth and seventeenth centuries, England in particular developed a sense of national peoplehood in which pride in a special inheritance of political liberty mingled with belief that the English enjoyed special divine favour as representatives of true religion (Greenfeld 1992: 60–77). In the eighteenth century a secularized version of this dual sense of privilege and responsibility became a justification for Britain's imperial mission. By that time the sense of chosenness had passed to America (O'Brien 1988; Smith 2003). No less than the Puritan colonists, the Founding Fathers and their successors saw in the achievements of their own people a promise for all mankind. In more recent times this sense that (in the words of John Schaar) America has 'a teaching mission among the nations' (Schaar 1981: 293) has generated a notably ideological foreign policy. More generously, it has contributed to the successful integration of the millions of diverse immigrants who entered America under the eye of the Statue of Liberty. But the irony of Liberty's universal words of welcome is that a mission to all people does not erase the boundary between the chosen people and the rest. The American people may be readier than the peoples of Europe to welcome new recruits, but the boundary between insiders and outsiders remains, denying to people in general the rights enjoyed by 'our' people. Neither liberal universalism nor globalization can erase the significance of these boundaries, though both make them harder to justify. To conclude this chapter on specific peoples and people in general, let us then turn to this conundrum of inclusion and exclusion.

Shutting the Door on People

Claims about citizenship draw our attention to our irreconcilably split identities as modern political subjects. As citizens, we want to be humans, to attribute our behaviour to universal norms of (ethical) conduct. But, as citizens, we are also always prepared to keep other humans out.

Rob Walker, 'Citizenship after the modern subject'

For vivid illustrations of the collision between the claims of people in general and the contingent borders of any particular people, we need only look at the increasingly desperate attempts by illegal immigrants and asylum-seekers to get into democratic countries, and the equally frantic attempts of the countries concerned to keep them out. The tensions involved are philosophically confusing, morally tormenting and politically explosive. Seen from outside, the polities concerned may seem merely hypocritical in professing universal principles while defending the privileged rights of their own peoples; insult is certainly added to injury when such polities lecture the rest of the world in the hectoring tone that goes with being a chosen people. But these inconsistencies should be seen as evidence not just of hypocrisy but of something more significant: the inescapable consequences of political contingency.

The basic problem is one that Rousseau hit on over two centuries ago. In a draft for what eventually became the *Social Contract*, he attacked Natural Law theory for what seemed to him its shallow and misleading assumption that universal moral and political principles must have been already obvious to human beings before the foundation of particular states. On the contrary, wrote Rousseau, it is only after experiencing the bonds of particular republics that we are able to imagine society on a larger scale, so that in a sense we become men only after having been citizens (Rousseau 1962, I: 453). Where cosmopolitans might nevertheless see a natural progression from narrower to wider sympathies, Rousseau recognized that these later, wider loyalties conflict with the demands of their home base; the obligations of man and citizen are at odds with one another (Rousseau 1911: 7). Rousseau was of course writing from within the tradition of the classical republican city-state, and the contrast between cosmopolitan ideals and the narrow virtue of his beloved Spartans was particularly sharp. The national peoples with which we are now familiar are much larger and more inclusive; nevertheless they are also *ex*clusive, with boundaries that a great many people would like to cross.

The crucial point is that this privileged boundedness, which seems so offensively inconsistent with the universal principles professed by liberal democrats, is at the same time the political precondition of those universal principles themselves. The principles of human rights arose in a few specific polities, and continue to need such a home base, even though they call its legitimacy into question. In a few fortunate locations, the experience of being a political people gave rise to the notion that all people everywhere should enjoy similar rights. The solidarity shared by peoples in the same few fortunate locations has generated enough collective power to guarantee the rights of 'our people', plus a surplus of power that can on occasion be projected abroad for the benefit of some people elsewhere (Canovan 1998). But political peoplehood and its benefits continue to be rare, patchy and attractive to outsiders; meanwhile the deceptive stability and security of these blessings makes their restriction to 'our people' seem even more morally offensive. How can the contingent reality of bounded, privileged peoples be reconciled with the universal ideal of equal rights for all people?[5]

It is possible to approach this dilemma from two opposite points of view, starting either from the universal ideals or else from the political contingencies – though the vital point to be borne in mind is that neither of these opposed perspectives can be ignored. Both are inescapably present within modern western political culture and political activity. The issue cannot, therefore, be satisfactorily dealt with as a clash between utopianism and realism, or between the morally sensitive and the obtuse.

If we look at the topic from the perspective of universalist ideals, the exclusionary boundaries of specific peoples seem not only contingent but arbitrary, illegitimate and outdated. Universalists concede that the liberal and democratic ideals associated with the notion of the people did indeed develop within the bounded communities of specific peoples, but argue that once developed, the ideals point beyond those boundaries. Alongside the increasingly widespread conviction that all people are equal in human rights, and that the people everywhere are the ultimate source of political legitimacy, globalization itself is strengthening the connections between people and reducing the significance of borders. The conclusion widely drawn from this conjunction of moral and empirical pressures is that old forms of bounded political community are being superseded, while new, all-inclusive forms are emerging and should be supported. Some cosmopolitans, including David Held and Daniele Archibugi, have put forward schemes for full-scale global democracy in the form of a strengthened United Nations that would incorporate a directly elected 'People's Assembly' (Archibugi and Held 1995; Holden 2000). Despite elaborate arrangements for intermediate layers of accountable government, the apparent aim is to take the familiar model of a government accountable to a specific sovereign people and to inflate it to the point where both government and people become all-inclusive.

Schemes as ambitious as that are striking but not entirely characteristic of the cosmopolitan literature. Rather than seeking to replace bounded popular sovereignty with the formal structure of a universal People's Democracy, many thinkers favour a more nuanced picture that emphasizes the fluidity of politics in a world where boundaries are blurred and sovereignty outdated. Rather than looking to a collective global People to speak through a formal People's Assembly, such accounts tend to lay stress on the ever-increasing networks of less formal contacts between individuals and groups that make up global civil society (Carter 2001; Hutchings and Dannreuther 1999). For Andrew Linklater, as for Jürgen Habermas, this reaching out in dialogue to 'the imagined community of humankind' is no less than 'the unfinished moral business of the sovereign state' (Linklater 1999: 36). Inside the borders of liberal democratic states, the moral impetus that first endowed citizens with rights has continued to push for more and more inclusive understandings of citizenship, extending new rights to women, the poor, ethnic minorities and others who were formerly excluded. For Linklater, the logic of this progression is clear: the next discriminatory barrier to be broken down is the boundary between insiders and outsiders. 'National populations . . . must be troubled by the practice of attaching as much moral significance to the difference between citizens and aliens as they used to impute to the differences of class, gender, ethnicity or race' (Linklater 1999: 48).

Cosmopolitans are right to draw attention to the combination of universal principles, expanding sympathies and globalizing trends that is putting in question the boundaries between specific peoples and people in general. But there is another side to this issue; we cannot afford to ignore the brute political contingencies left out of this exalted vision. However hard it may be in the abstract to justify a boundary between 'our people' and outsiders, political discussion has to start from the fact that such boundaries are in place. They are indeed *increasing* in political salience, not only because of globalization and the migration and international terrorism it brings, but also because the ever-increasing rights citizens enjoy makes insider status ever more valuable. Neither can such boundaries be considered inconsistent with democracy, since they are in one sense democracy's precondition and in another sense its outcome. On the one hand democracy requires a political community; as David Miller points out in his critique of the notion of cosmopolitan citizenship, all political experience so far suggests that effective citizenship is possible only in a bounded polity with a sense of distinct identity, republican or national (Miller 1999). It is hard to imagine enough popular solidarity at a global level to allow a United Nations 'People's Assembly' to hold the global government to account.

Furthermore, that necessarily bounded democratic people will insist on being consulted about constitutional and territorial changes. Peoples usually want to maintain a distinction between insiders and outsiders; schemes for full-blown 'global democracy' collapse as soon as one tries to imagine the American people voting to hand over power to a strengthened United Nations. Neither could any political party in a democratic state win an election by promising to open the borders to all comers. This is not to say that democratic electorates are immune to the widening of sympathies described by Linklater and others. The criteria for who counts as 'one of us' are highly contingent and variable over time. In the USA, notions of who can truly be regarded as belonging to the American people have widened dramatically over the course of the Republic's history. And although no European people so far exists, many EU citizens who would once have been regarded as outsiders in one another's states no longer seem to be so. It would be rash to read too much into this, however, because one of the reasons for it is simply that the boundaries between insiders and outsiders have been redrawn in a different place. Italians in France or English in Ireland may seem like honorary insiders when compared with more exotic incomers.

Although opposition to immigration may often be based on ignorance, racial prejudice and negative stereotypes, from the point of view of democracy it cannot be regarded as entirely irrational. Democracy is rare; the people of a democratic polity are privileged possessors of something that is precious and fragile – perhaps even (borrowing from the language of chosen peoplehood) a trust for humanity. Depending on their scale and nature, demographic changes could have politically disastrous effects. While a handful of migrants from whatever background is likely to have little effect for good or ill, a sudden influx into (say) Australia of twenty million people from a non-democratic political culture would certainly cause violent conflict and might destroy democracy altogether. Somewhere between the two extremes lie a range of practical possibilities to be found in the course of political struggles and accommodations; and yet the fact remains that the means required to implement unavoidable border controls – the camps and deportations and presumption of guilt – fly in the face of universal principles and continually affront liberal democratic consciences (Barry and Goodin 1992).

This tension between the requirements of a bounded people and the claims of people in general haunts modern liberal democracy. Since the Second World War, the political classes within liberal democracies have tended to be more cosmopolitan in their views than voters at the grass roots. European elites in particular tried for many years to keep issues such as immigration off the political agenda, and to exclude politically incorrect views about outsiders from political discourse. One of the striking political developments of the past decade has been a populist reaction purporting to be a movement of the people, and focused particularly on migration and the borders between insiders and outsiders. Seeking to mobilize 'ordinary people' against the holders of power, such movements appeal to the solidarity of the people as a nation and take their stand on the rights of the people as ultimate sovereign. The populism they exemplify is the subject of the next chapter.

4

Part and Whole: People, Populism and Democracy

> I was not put on the ballot by either of the two parties . . . This is a movement that came from the people. This is the way the framers of the Constitution intended our government to be, a government that comes from the people.
>
> Ross Perot in Westlind 1996

We have seen that even if 'the people' is understood in relatively inclusive terms, its borders remain problematic because the notion implies a bounded polity, yet points beyond that to humanity at large. When we turn from those problems of external definition to focus on the people *inside* a single polity, we are once again faced with theoretical ambiguities and practical tensions. Internally, the theoretical peculiarity is that 'the people' has always had two apparently incompatible senses, meaning either the whole polity or one part of the population – sometimes the privileged part that controlled the polity, but more often the part excluded from power. The stubborn ambiguity between part and whole has persisted through many political conflicts in which the people-as-excluded-part have claimed power as the largest section of the people-as-sovereign-whole.

Within contemporary western politics, populist movements still seek to mobilize the people as excluded part in the name of the people as sovereign whole, and their demand is still that power must be taken from the elite and given to the people. In the US presidential election of 1992, Ross Perot attracted 19 per cent of the popular vote for his campaign to let the people take back control of the people's government. As the quotation at the head of this chapter indicates, that enterprise seemed to him a simple matter of recalling the Constitution to its original principles. To many observers, however, his movement, like parallel movements in other established democracies, seemed alarmingly populist rather than reassuringly democratic. As we shall see, confusion about the relationship between populism and democracy is entangled with the people's internal dialectic of part and whole.

The problem of defining 'populism' will be addressed later in this chapter, but many of those so labelled understand it as the people's struggle to redeem the promise of popular sovereignty. We saw in chapter 2 that democratic reform in Britain and the USA was fuelled by belief in the sovereignty of the people as a whole, a principle constantly invoked by the 'common people' as they fought for full inclusion in their polity. There are, however, less comfortable aspects to the relation between populism and democracy. Mobilization of the common people may have played a crucial role in the history of liberal democracy, but it has also been associated with revolutionary violence and with the emergence of populist dictators. In most societies prior to the twentieth century the common people were sharply distinguished from the elite, forming not just a numerical majority but a mass that was poor, ignorant and despised. Even when legitimized by the political doctrine of popular sovereignty, their struggles were concerned with wealth and honour as well as power. Those struggles, sharpened by the resentment of the humiliated, sometimes allowed demagogues and dictators to ride to power.

Commentators fearing for the safety of liberal democracy have tended to see disturbing continuities between past and present. And yet the 'New Populism' represented by Ross Perot and others presents modern democrats with a different kind of conundrum. The contemporary western polities stirred by calls for the people to reclaim their sovereign power no longer contain a subordinate and distinct 'common people'. It is true that populists draw a contrast between professional politicians and 'ordinary people', but the latter are a diffuse and amorphous electorate, used to being wooed by politicians obsessed by opinion polls. How can there be scope for mobilization to 'take back' the people's government in stable, well-established liberal democracies like the USA, Canada, Australia and Western Europe?

The increasing incidence of populist politics within liberal democracies has puzzled many commentators, and we shall see later that a variety of explanations have been offered. The principal concern of this chapter is, however, with the ambiguous resonances of 'the people' as part and whole, and the political responses they allow or invite. The structure of the chapter is as follows. Section 1 sketches the history of the 'common people' and the links binding popular mobilization to liberal democracy on the one hand and populist dictatorship on the other. In section 2 the focus shifts to contemporary populism, especially the 'New Populist' movements that have recently been challenging the political conventions of liberal democracies. Section 3 considers the more general problem of defining 'populism'. What makes movements 'populist', according to a number of analysts, is not their programme or constituency but a common discourse centred on recapturing power for the sovereign people. Significant support for movements of this kind in polities with all the trappings of liberal democracy therefore prompts awkward questions. Should populists (whose avowed aim is to take power from the politicians and restore it to the people) be seen as the true democrats they claim to be? Or are they (as their critics claim) dangerous enemies of liberal democracy?

A persuasive response to these questions (favoured particularly by European analysts) is that democracy as we know it in modern polities is an uneasy combination of two different strands, populist democracy and liberal constitutionalism. New Populism sets the cat among the pigeons by threatening to upset the balance between the two strands. This 'two strand' theory of populism and its relation to democracy will be considered in section 4 below. I shall argue that despite its considerable plausibility the theory is misleading in two respects. In the first place it exaggerates the opposition between liberal constitutionalism and the cause of 'the people', ignoring the many historic links between them. Secondly, it distracts attention from crucial issues raised by populist rhetoric concerning 'the people' as ultimate source of political authority. Populist rhetoric puts the sovereign people in the spotlight, but it makes their nature, authority and power to act seem quite simple and straightforward. Nothing could be further from the truth. I shall argue that 'the people' should indeed be brought out of the shadows, in the hope of shedding light on its deep obscurities.

1   The Common People

In his account of *Politics in the Ancient World*, Moses Finley speaks of 'the ambiguity of the word *demos* . . . on the one hand, it meant the citizen body as a whole . . .; on the other hand it meant the common people, the many, the poor . . . The Latin *populus* had the same double connotation' (Finley 1983: 1). That ancient citizen population was itself a select group, raised above slaves, women and foreign residents. As Aristotle stressed, however, the *demos* in the sense of the majority of citizens meant the poor as opposed to the rich (Aristotle 1992: 192, 245, 269). In Republican Rome, *populus* in this sense meant the *plebs*, who were despised and often feared by their patrician betters. Three connected reasons for fearing the common people were passed on to later political thinkers. Since the people were the poor, they could easily be incited by demagogues to plunder the rich. Being also ignorant and resentful, they were irrational and liable to turn into a mob, the 'many-headed monster' that haunted elite political imagination from Plato to Shakespeare and beyond (Hill 1974). They posed a danger to any mixed constitution and limits on power because, thirdly, they could be induced by a populist military leader to support the establishment of a tyranny – the phenomenon dubbed 'Caesarism' after Julius Caesar's rise to personal power by wooing the *plebs* with bread and circuses (Baehr 1998).

The classical legacy on the subject of the people was therefore very mixed. We saw in chapter 2 that Roman thinking about the sovereign *populus* was itself passed down in a deeply ambiguous form; alongside those confused and exalted notions of the people-as-whole political community, however, lay the dark shadow of 'the common people'. When struggles between King and Parliament in seventeenth-century England gave the principle of popular sovereignty a new prominence, those who used it found themselves embarrassed because these two senses of 'people' seemed to point in opposite directions. In their more honourable guise as the sovereign political community, the people were fit to call kings to account; but it was hard to use the term without calling up alarming visions of the mass of the population. The gentry might see themselves as the natural representatives of the whole political community, but once popular sovereignty had been invoked against the King, the principle could be used by the Levellers to claim political rights for the excluded in the name of the people as a whole.

Attempts by Royalists to discredit the notion of popular sovereignty by interpreting it as mob rule led some Whig gentlemen to try to dissociate it from the common people. One early eighteenth-century republican and defender of the people's liberty, Thomas Gordon, was particularly outspoken:

> by the People I mean not the idle and indigent rabble, under which name the People are often understood and traduced, but all who have property, without the privileges of Nobility . . . (Gordon 1737, III: 191)

By the mid-eighteenth century, however, that harsh clarity was unusual in England. More common was a vaguer, more malleable discourse within which the common people (who were, after all, members of the English *national* people) were included within the sovereign people, though they were supposed to be naturally represented by their betters. The radical potentialities of this discourse were obvious to some in England and to more in America. If the people as a whole are sovereign, and if the common people make up the bulk of that whole people, then there is surely a prima facie case for the common people to claim political rights. The American Revolution gave radicals the opportunity to press the case for electoral inclusion within the polity of (male, white) members of the common people. In nineteenth-century Britain the same cause was pursued over a much longer period by a series of movements, notably the Chartists and the Liberal Party.

Contrary to classical precedents, radical mobilization of the common people in America turned out after all to be compatible with constitutional balance, while in nineteenth-century Britain it turned out to be reformist rather than revolutionary. But this was in no sense a foregone conclusion, so that the fears of many in the privileged classes were not unreasonable. The French Revolution associated the cause of the common people not with civil liberty and limited government but with revolutionary violence, expropriation, tyranny and Caesarism. As in the days of Aristotle, the common people were still the poor, and their campaign for full incorporation in a polity based on popular sovereignty was also a class struggle against the rich. It is worth pausing for a moment to consider how this 'populist' mobilization of the common people differed from the familiar Marxist picture of class-conflict, especially in Britain, the country that inspired that vision.

The first difference is that the populist social radicalism of the late eighteenth and early nineteenth centuries was addressed (as in earlier times) to a wide and loosely defined constituency. Instead of Marx's new industrial proletariat, a more varied collection of artisans, craftsmen and others were attracted to radical groups that used the broad and inclusive discourse of 'the people' (Calhoun 1982; Stedman Jones 1983; Joyce 1991). Where Marxist analysis was economistic, populist radicalism was political in the sense of attributing economic ills to political causes and seeking political remedies such as the vote. Populists justified their radicalism by appealing to the familiar principle of popular sovereignty, and this difference in legitimation was associated with a completely different attitude to history. In Marxist theory proletarians were the progressive class, created by technological change and destined to inherit its fruits. But the populist radicalism of early nineteenth-century England and other industrializing societies was more often associated with resistance to change and defence of the traditional communities and way of life of the common people. The classic populist radical in English history is the early nineteenth-century journalist and agitator, William Cobbett, a deeply conservative figure who articulated popular hostility to what he and others saw as oppression of the people by an increasingly corrupt elite. Marx might see existing states simply as tools of capitalism, but Cobbett and his like believed that they were struggling to regain possession of a free constitution that was by right already theirs. Excluded and oppressed as the common people might be, they were conscious of forming the vast majority of that sovereign people to whom rightful power belonged. Analysis, strategy and legitimacy all relied on the concept of 'the people', and especially on its ambiguity between sovereign whole and excluded part.

Because so much populist radicalism in nineteenth-century Britain aimed at inclusion in the existing parliamentary system, an accommodation with the liberal democratic reform movement proved eventually to be possible. French experience, by contrast, seemed to confirm classical fears about the consequences of mobilizing the common people. Reaping the fruits of popular revolution, Napoleons I and III legitimized their empires by plebiscite, appealing to the principle of popular sovereignty and to the votes of the common people. Following in their footsteps, charismatic leaders in a variety of countries have since used their rapport with the common people to help them subvert liberal democracy. Populism's dubious reputation in Europe has a great deal to do with memories of Adolf Hitler's talent for mass mobilization. Outside Europe, more or less dictatorial populist leaders have been particularly common in Latin America, where charismatic figures from Juan and Eva Peron to Hugo Chavez have gained power by mobilizing the urban poor against a rich elite. Latin American Populism has often been diagnosed as a symptom of 'backwardness' characteristic of imperfectly modernized regions on the fringes of the rich world, a transitional phase on the bumpy road to liberal democratic politics (e.g. Di Tella 1997: 199, 190; cf. Laclau 1979).

Like classical and early nineteenth-century mobilizations of the common people, the movements called 'populist' in Latin America have usually been urban, addressed to the most visible and vocal of the underdogs. But the supposed link between 'populism' and 'backwardness' may seem all the more plausible when we consider that the former term first came into use in the late nineteenth century to describe two (unconnected) radical movements aimed at rural 'people' – peasants in Russia, farmers in America. The Russian *Narodnichestvo* (usually translated 'populism') was an abortive revolutionary movement among young intellectuals inspired by idealized notions of peasant life. In the 1870s they 'went to the people' expecting to stir up rebellion against the Tsar and the landed class and to establish communal ownership of the land (Venturi 1960; Wortman 1967). On that occasion their project found little response, but in the following half-century peasant movements across Eastern Europe (often with charismatic leaders, and some of them influenced by *narodnik* ideas) did at times succeed in articulating a distinctive radicalism that addressed peasants' economic interests, idealized their way of life and used the discourse of 'the people' to do so (Canovan 1981: 112–28; Mudde 2002). It is a matter of historical accident that East European peasant radicals should share the title of 'populist' with Latin American dictators; despite huge differences, however, similarities may perhaps be found if one concentrates on the mobilization of down-trodden people in societies that are (in some rather elastic sense) economically 'backward'. With a certain amount of strain, both phenomena might then be fitted into a story of the common people that would stretch back to Caesar and to Aristotle, taking in peasant revolts along the way. But that story is hard to connect with the current upsurge of so-called 'populism' in modern western politics. A tenuous link can be made via the other classic case, nineteenth-century American Populism, but only at the cost of some contentious interpretation of history (McMath 1993: 9–16).

The term 'populist' became established in English primarily to describe those who chose to call themselves by this name – the members of the US People's Party, formed in the 1890s as the culmination of a decade of agrarian radicalism. Unlike the peasants idealized by the *Narodniki*, most American Populists were commercial farmers producing commodities for distant markets. The targets of their wrath were their creditors, the railroad corporations on which they depended to carry their crops, the scarce gold currency that depressed farm prices and inflated their debts, and (echoing Jacksonian attacks on 'the money power') the plutocrats of Wall Street who wallowed in luxury while hard-working producers struggled to make ends meet. This was a grass roots movement without a charismatic leader, and one of its notable features was faith in popular government as established by the

US Constitution. Like Cobbett and the English radicals of the early nineteenth century (and indeed like the Levellers of seventeenth-century England) the Populists saw themselves simply as the sovereign people, organized to take back what was rightfully theirs. The platform adopted at the party's first nominating convention, held in Omaha in July 1892, declared, 'We seek to restore the government of the Republic to the hands of "the plain people" with whose class it originated' (Hicks 1961: 441). The conviction that they were not a special interest but were speaking for the overwhelming mass of the people emerges clearly from their rhetoric:

> I will tell you what you are going to see ... You will see arrayed on one side the great magnates of the country, and Wall Street brokers, and the plutocratic power; and on the other you will see the people. (Goodwyn 1976: 192)

The high point of the movement was the 1892 presidential election, in which the Populist candidate James Weaver polled over a million votes.

American Populism can in some ways be seen as a link between traditional movements of 'the common people' and mobilization of 'ordinary people' by contemporary populists. This may account for the conflicting interpretations the movement has received from historians. Its base in agrarian poverty and its demonization of Wall Street have encouraged some to fit it into a story of 'backwardness' that can be linked to the populisms of peasants and Latin American dictators, a story that is also a cautionary tale about the dangers of populist irrationality (Hofstadter 1968: 62–93). But the Populists' political discourse and programme put them into different company and raised different questions. In a sympathetic account of the emergence of their movement from the grass roots, Lawrence Goodwyn saw them as exemplary democrats intent on bringing popular sovereignty to life by putting control of the people's government in the people's hands (Goodwyn 1976). That is precisely the rallying call of contemporary populists, who also claim to be true democrats. How are we to make sense of these conflicting signals and how should we respond to contemporary invocations of 'the people'? Should we see them as democracy in action or as a threat to democracy? To be able to address these questions we first need to make a more sustained effort to clarify what 'populism' means. The next two sections look first at the movements labelled 'populist' in contemporary liberal democratic polities and then at the broader problem of identifying and analysing 'populism' in general.

2   Populism in Contemporary Liberal Democracies

Use of the term by journalists and political scientists often gives the impression that 'populism' is widespread in contemporary politics. Within liberal democracies the label is attached to two sorts of phenomena, one of which causes alarm while the other is more apt to induce cynicism. The latter, perhaps best called 'politicians' populism', will be discussed later in this section; for the former, which has mushroomed in the past couple of decades, I shall adopt Paul Taggart's label, 'New Populism' (Taggart 1995).[1]

New Populism

Many liberal democracies have recently seen the emergence of movements that challenge existing parties and mainstream policies (Taggart 1995, 2000). Typically confrontational in style, they claim to represent the rightful source of legitimate power – the people, whose interests and wishes have been ignored by self-interested politicians and politically correct intellectuals. These challengers do not in general call themselves 'populists', and despite some links they have not so far seen themselves as branches of an international ideological movement in the way that (for example) Greens do. Claiming in each case to speak for a particular national people, they are not natural internationalists. But although there are many differences between their policy prescriptions, they do share a distinctive style and message. Many of these movements have been short-lived and others marginal, but collectively their political impact has already been considerable, particularly in Europe. Cases generally recognized as falling into this category, despite many differences, include Ross Perot's 1992 presidential campaign in the USA, Pauline Hanson's One Nation Party in Australia, and Preston Manning's Reform Party in Canada. Of the many European cases, the most long-lasting is Jean Marie Le Pen's *Front Nationale* in France; other particularly conspicuous examples include Jörg Haider's Freedom Party in Austria; Umberto Bossi's Northern League in Italy, and the brief eruption in the Netherlands of the movement led by Pim Fortuyn. Fortuyn's assassination just before the Dutch general election in 2002 dramatically illustrated one of the typical features of these New Populist movements, their overwhelming dependence on personal leadership rather than institutional party structures.

When these leaders and parties are called 'populist' the term may be used analytically or pejoratively. In neutral terms they can be said to be populist in the sense that their *raison d'être is* an appeal to 'the people' against that people's supposed representatives. Drawing on the principle that the people are sovereign, they accuse professional politicians and opinion formers of neglecting the interests and values of the mass of the people of their particular polity. But that kind of appeal to the grass roots also attracts the label 'populist' in a derogatory sense, linked to the history of the common people traced earlier. In Continental Europe the term often carries echoes of popular irrationality and manipulative leadership, reminiscent of Hitler's racist demagogy. Liberal commentators worry not only about the prominence of charismatic leaders within the new movements but especially about the popular sentiments they have most successfully highlighted, hostility to mass immigration and to multiculturalism. 'Populism' in the pejorative sense is therefore taken to mean 'right-wing extremism'. Where immigration is concerned, most New Populists can indeed be located at the Right of the traditional political spectrum (Betz 1994). But the case of Pim Fortuyn in the Netherlands showed that such labels can be misleading. Nor only was Fortuyn openly gay (and therefore anathema to many on the Right) but his reasons for opposing Muslim immigration and multicultural policies found some echoes on the Left. In that particular case – in the context of a liberal popular culture – the populist claim to speak for the people against their supposed representatives could not simply be dismissed as right-wing xenophobia (*The Economist*, 4 May 2002: 14–16).

Claiming to speak for the forgotten mass of ordinary people, New Populists necessarily take on the colour of their surroundings (Taggart 2000). The positions they campaign for and the values they express depend on local concerns and the kind of political establishment they are challenging. Invariably critical of professional politicians and the media, they claim to say aloud what the people think, especially if it has been deemed by the elite to be unmentionable. New Populists often call for issues of popular concern to be decided by referendum, bypassing professional politicians and leaving decisions to the people. By way of emphasizing their closeness to the grass roots and their distance from the political establishment they also tend to use colourful and undiplomatic language. They are most comfortable in opposition, though some have had enough electoral success to find themselves sharing power. The strength of the populist challenge to established liberal democratic politics was most dramatically symbolized by the success of Jean Marie Le Pen in reaching the second, decisive round in the 2002 French presidential election. Le Pen, one of the most uncompromisingly right-wing and nationalist of all the New Populists, managed to defeat the outgoing Socialist prime minister in the first ballot, obliging the French Left (whose divisions had made this possible) to support their old enemy President Chirac in the second ballot to keep Le Pen out of power (*The Economist*, 27 April 2002: 25–7; cf. Surel 2002).

'New Populism' has attracted a good deal of attention from commentators and analysts because of the challenge it appears to pose to the practice and theory of contemporary democratic politics. Le Pen, Haider and their like are even believed by some to threaten the subversion of liberal democracy. Yet New Populists take their stand on the sovereignty of the people and claim that they themselves are the true democrats, defending that people against an unresponsive elite. The theoretical problem is therefore to understand the tense relationship between populism and democracy, an issue that will be taken up in the final section of this chapter. In the meantime we need to explore another sort of 'populism' that is current in some western polities. This is a style of politics that is in some ways very different from New Populism, although the two sometimes overlap because they draw on a common political discourse of 'the people'. A convenient label for it is 'Politicians' Populism'.

Politicians' Populism

One of the reasons for current confusion about the meaning of 'populism' is that besides being used to describe the confrontational politics that mobilizes ordinary people against those inside the establishment, the term also refers to a classic tactic available to political insiders, a kind of 'catch-all' politics that sets out to appeal to the people as a whole. Like New Populism, this kind of politics is often highly personalized. A professional politician who is an effective communicator sets out to appeal across old demarcations, playing down divisions along the lines of party, class or ideology and stressing the unity of the whole people. In the USA, which escaped many of the conflicts over class and ideology from which European party systems emerged, there has long been scope for this sort of populism alongside periodic upsurges of the more confrontational, anti-establishment kind. The discourse of appeals to 'the people' is indeed so thoroughly domesticated in American political culture that 'populism' has fewer derogatory associations in the USA than in Europe, allowing professional politicians actually to claim the title. As Alan Ware observes, populism there 'forms one aspect of the political mainstream' (Ware 2002: 119).

Outside the USA, Politicians' Populism is associated more with the weakening of traditional party structures, now that divisions based on class and ideology have less salience and modern media have taken us into an era of what Bernard Manin calls 'audience democracy' (Manin 1997: 220). Television maximizes the importance of personal leadership, allowing and encouraging leaders to appeal to the electorate as a whole while bypassing party structures and the ideological commitments they embody. The inclusive language of 'the people' has been much used by Tony Blair, who successfully repackaged Britain's Labour Party as 'New Labour', shorn of its exclusively socialist and working-class

associations. Discussing 'Blairism', Peter Mair speaks of populism as 'a form of governing in which party is sidelined or
disappears; where the people are undifferentiated, and in
which a more or less "neutral" government attempts to serve
the interests of all' (Mair 2002: 96). Although catch-all politics from above may seem a totally different matter from anti-
establishment crusades from the grass roots, both use a
discourse laying stress on 'the people' understood as a single
body with common interests. The case of Italy's Silvio
Berlusconi shows that it is possible to make the transition
from anti-establishment crusader to catch-all leader, at any
rate in a polity like Italy where the old party system had
become thoroughly discredited (Tarchi 2002).

   Within contemporary western polities, New Populism may
alarm liberals and Politicians' Populism prompt cynicism but
neither seems to pose an imminent threat to constitutional
or to economic stability. Elsewhere, in different political and
socio-economic circumstances, mobilization of the excluded
people may carry a more subversive agenda. Charismatic leadership may burst the bonds of constitutional legality, while
'the people' mobilized as a class may be economically radical,
if only in the sense of supporting the protectionist, inflation-
ary 'macroeconomic populism' often seen in Latin America in
the past (Dornbusch and Edwards 1990). The memory and
continuing possibility of movements that fall into one or
another of these categories of 'populism' adds to the confusion in current use of the term.

3   Identifying Populism

Study of populism has been hampered by the difficulty of
finding clear connecting links between the different senses in
which the term is used. While some analysts have offered def-
initions or listed essential characteristics of populism, others
have found only more tenuous connections and loose family
resemblances between the different populisms; in all cases,
attempts at a general characterization have been contentious
(Ionescu and Gellner 1969; Laclau 1979; Canovan 1981,
1982; Westlind 1996; Taggart 2000). The term's form suggests affinities with ideological movements like socialism,

liberalism or nationalism. But although all these other 'isms' range over widely varied phenomena, each gains a degree of coherence from a continuous history, willingness on the part of most adherents to identify themselves by the name, distinctive principles and policies. Populism does not fit this pattern. There is no acknowledged common history, ideology, programme or social base, and the term is usually applied to movements from outside, often as a term of abuse. Members of the US People's Party were unusual in calling themselves 'Populists', for most of those conventionally given the label do not themselves embrace it. It is hard to imagine there being any mutual acknowledgement of political kinship between (say) Tony Blair, Hugo Chavez and Jean Marie Le Pen, nor the three of them joining in common veneration of ancestors among the *narodniki* and the US People's Party. As Paul Taggart says, the term 'populism' has 'an awkward conceptual slipperiness' (Taggart 2000: 1).

While overlaps and family resemblances can be found between some of the phenomena that have for one reason or another attracted the label, across the board they seem to have little in common apart from a rhetoric of appeals to 'the people' (Canovan 1981, 1982, 1984).[2] Recent studies have underlined the importance of that populist discourse and shown that paying more attention to it can help both in understanding particular cases and in analysing populist phenomena more generally (e.g. Kazin 1995; Westlind 1996; Laclau 2005). Once attention has been focused on discourses of 'the people', the next step is to investigate the range of meanings made available to populists by 'the people's' ambiguities. An important advance along this path has been made by Yves Mény and Yves Surel in their analysis of New Populist movements. Underlining the importance in populism of appeals to the people, Mény and Surel identify three overlapping senses in which that 'people' is invoked: as rightful sovereign, as downtrodden class and as nation (Mény and Surel 2000). While acknowledging linguistic differences between *peuple, Volk* and 'people', however, their Francophone analysis leaves out the extra complications associated with 'the people's' distinctively Anglophone ambiguity between individual political actors and a collective sovereign in reserve.

Mény and Surel link their threefold conception of the people as sovereign, class and nation with three areas of concern that can provide bases for mobilization: matters of politics, economics and culture (Mény and Surel 2000: 185). If (as I have argued) 'the people's' ambiguities go beyond the former trinity, the latter categorization may be too neat to be altogether convincing. It is nevertheless helpful to look at these three dimensions of discontent when trying to come to grips not only with New Populism but with the vast range of diverse 'populisms' that have in one way or another made use of mobilizing discourses of 'the people'. Populist mobilizations are usually linked to popular economic grievances of some kind; they normally have some sort of cultural dimension concerned with defending the people's values, and they are invariably political, claiming power for the people. Each of these themes allows for a range of variations, while the various themes have themselves been intermingled in many different ways. What links them together and identifies them all (however tenuously) as 'populist' is the broad and variable discourse of 'the people'.

The many different ways in which 'the people', their interests and their antagonists have been conceived make it futile to try to identify populism with any particular programme or social base. Nevertheless, what all populisms have in common is an appeal to the notion of 'the people' as ultimate source of legitimacy, and it is this appeal that makes New Populism both potent and problematic. The affluent liberal democracies in which they have been springing up lack many of the classic bases for populist mobilization. Such societies are no longer polarized by the old economic division between common people and rich elite; there is no mass of peasants, nor even a rural majority. Indeed the collapse of the old class structures into less stratified and more diverse social forms makes it harder for populist entrepreneurs to identify economic interests and concerns that are salient to large sections of the population. Culturally, the mass of the population are no longer excluded from education or openly despised, while the mass media aim at the widest possible audience. Above all, on the political dimension these are states with popular government, not only legitimized by the principle of popular consent but with rulers accountable to the entire population in free elections. The political elite is wider than ever before and largely composed of politicians who court the voters and resort to populist language themselves. How is it possible, then, for an increasing number of movements to gain a hearing for their message of recapturing power for the people, reasserting the people's values and defending the people's economic interests?

These questions are not altogether new, for they have surfaced periodically ever since the first establishment in the USA of a 'people's government'. Even in the 1830s Jacksonian Democrats were being mobilized, like New Populists, to 'take back power' supposedly stolen from the people. The regular recurrence of this theme suggests that it may be rooted in the very nature of modern democracy, providing a stimulus to mobilization more long-lasting than the specific grievances that set off populist movements at particular places and times. Before addressing that broader issue of the relation between populism and democracy we need to take note of some more specific explanations that have been offered for the rise of New Populism.

Although populism has occasionally persuaded a few intellectuals to turn on their own order and throw in their lot with the people,[3] relations between populists and the academy have seldom been comfortable. This can make it hard for analysts to view such movements objectively. Where earlier generations of cultured gentlemen looked at action by the common people and saw 'the beast with many heads', so political scientists have been tempted to treat more recent populist movements as pathological symptoms of some social disease rather than political phenomena to be understood on their own terms (e.g. Betz 1994, 2002; Immerfall 1998).

No doubt this approach has some validity; there may indeed be few political activists (of any stripe) whose motivations would stand up well to scrutiny. But Mény and Surel are surely right to argue that while such considerations may help us to understand populism, they do not excuse us from paying attention to its political and ideological aspects. From that point of view New Populism embodies a political challenge to existing democratic systems, a challenge summed up in three propositions:

1   the people are the foundation of the community;
2   they have been robbed of their rightful primacy;

3 they must be restored to their proper place and society regenerated (Mény and Surel 2000: 181).

Why is it, then, that political claims of this kind have been attracting support within mature polities with elaborate arrangements for popular participation? A number of local or specific political circumstances have undoubtedly helped to set off populist movements. In Austria, for example, Jörg Haider's claim that parties and governments had lost touch with the people (Haider 1995: 88) struck a chord with many voters because a long tradition of 'cartel politics' had allowed power and its spoils to be monopolized by a permanent coalition of the two main parties (Müller 2002). A more profound distrust of Italian politicians, confirmed in the 1990s by revelations of wholesale corruption, provided a launching pad for populist movements (Tarchi 2002). Mény and Surel attribute a widespread 'crisis of political legitimacy' to corruption of an increasingly systematic kind carried on to fund political parties, allowing populists in several countries to argue with some plausibility that the entire representative system is rotten (Mény and Surel 2000: 167). Parties' financial problems have themselves been connected with changes in the relationship between voters and political elites. The party structures that used to link politicians to grass roots members are falling into decay, their place filled by television, which is not only ruinously expensive but inexorably personalizes politics. As the style and discourse of mainstream politicians verges more and more on 'Politicians' Populism', it is scarcely surprising that more confrontational populists should see opportunities (Mény and Surel 2000: 85).

If they are to make effective use of whatever institutional channels may be available, confrontational populists need to play on popular concerns that are not being addressed by the people's existing representatives. The salience of particular grievances varies from one country to another, but common themes include high taxes, unemployment, strains on the welfare state, crime and (increasingly) immigration and its consequences. As a spur to populist antagonism, these have been sharpened by constraints on elected governments' responsiveness to popular pressure, constraints imposed (particularly in the European Union) by a combination of constitutional commitments and liberal ideology.

Popular discontents to do with the defence of 'our people' in the face of immigration, asylum-seeking and multiculturalism have highlighted these constraints in Europe. The issue was dramatized by the outcome of Austria's 1999 elections. Jörg Haider's populist Freedom Party, the FPÖ, which had played on these discontents in its election campaign, emerged level with the second of the two previously dominant parties, the ÖVP. When the latter invited it into a coalition government, the leaders of Austria's EU partners declared this unacceptable because the FPÖ contravened the common liberal values of the European Union. Although a way of resolving the dispute was eventually found, this 'unprecedented attempt to intervene in the domestic politics of a fellow member state' (Müller 2002: 156) appeared to illustrate a tension in liberal democracy between popular sovereignty on the one hand and constitutional commitments informed by liberal values on the other. Seen from the populist perspective, the lesson was that so-called liberal democracies are not democratic at all. Whatever the people's choice, their decision can be overruled if it breaks a taboo on a sensitive subject.

The deeper issue raised by particular confrontations of this kind concerns the nature of democracy and its relation to populism. How is it that populists who are widely regarded as threats to democracy can claim that they themselves are the real democrats, expressing what the people really think and articulating concerns ignored by politicians but close to the people's hearts (cf. Le Pen, in Marcus 1995: 54)?

4 Populism, Democracy and the People

According to a good deal of recent discussion, New Populist movements should be seen not just as responses to specific political and socio-economic conditions but as evidence of tensions at the heart of modern liberal democracy. Analyses of these tensions vary, but the dominant theme is that democracy as we know it is a complex hybrid within which two essentially incompatible strands coexist. One is the populist agenda of popular sovereignty, 'power to the people', 'government of the people, by the people, for the people'. But (according to the analysis) that populist strand is balanced by a liberal constitutionalist strand, and the danger of populism is that it threatens this precarious balance. As Mény and Surel observe, 'All populist movements speak and behave as if democracy meant the power of the people and *only* the power of the people' (Mény and Surel 2002: 9).

Illuminating though it is, this two-strand analysis is in some ways misleading. For one thing it gives the impression that the populist and liberal strands in liberal democracy are essentially separate and antithetical. From an Anglophone perspective that is not the case. A more important disadvantage of the two-strand theory is, however, that its exclusive focus on liberal fears diverts attention from crucial issues raised by the appearance of populist movements in democratic polities, issues to do with the nature and authority of the sovereign people. In claiming power for the people and calling on those people to redeem the polity, populists are highlighting fundamental assumptions of contemporary politics: that the ultimate source of authority is the sovereign people; that all legitimate political power is based on the consent of the people, and that the people are capable on occasion of withdrawing legitimacy from one regime and bestowing it upon another.

Populist insistence on these truisms of modern political culture inadvertently shows up their embarrassing obscurity. For the 'people' whose authority is in question is/are not only fuzzy around the edges, as we have seen; its/their very constitution is in question. Any particular sovereign people – for example 'We, the People of the United States' – must somehow manage to be both a continuing, authoritative collective entity and a population of distinct individuals living and voting at a particular time. Can such a people be clearly conceived? Can it/they exist and act? Or does the people as sovereign authority belong within the realm of political myth, taking on vivid life in the overheated imaginations of populists and revolutionaries but in ordinary times acting as a necessary fiction for mass democracies? In the latter part of this section I shall argue that populist rhetoric should alert us to such neglected issues of democratic legitimacy. First, though, we need to consider the strengths and weaknesses of the 'two-strand' theory of populism's relation to liberal democracy.

Modern democracy is an exceedingly complex set of political practices and discourses, institutions and ideas. It includes constitutional limitation of the exercise of power in order to protect rights, including the rights of unpopular minorities. It also implies government conducted in accordance with liberal principles, sometimes contrary to popular opinion (Mény and Surel 2002: 7–10). Its sheer complexity offers a standing invitation to populists to insist on returning power to the people, while denouncing as undemocratic all complicating institutional and legal structures (Canovan 2002a). But if it is characteristic of populists to oversimplify modern democracy, their critics are tempted to underestimate its complexity in a rather different way. The temptation is to think of modern liberal democracy as a cross between two elements that are in essence quite different from one another: on the one hand, pure democracy, understood as direct rule by the people; on the other hand constitutional liberalism, conceived as an aristocratic tradition of limited government, primarily concerned with the protection of rights. The constitutional liberal strand in the model, associated with individual freedom as well as unequal property, is thought of as essentially opposed to popular power, which is associated in the model with mob rule and the tyranny of the majority. And since 'the people' are apparently on one side while freedom, rights and civilization are on the other, modern democracy has on this view been made possible only by drastically curbing popular access to politics. In a sense, then, the populists are right to see in contemporary democracy a conspiracy to keep power from the people, and they are dangerous precisely because they are right.[4] It is not difficult to find evidence that seems to support this two-strand analysis. Anyone wishing to tell the story of modern democracy as the bridling of populism by liberal-constitutionalism can point, for example, to the American Constitution, which was designed partly to protect property and civilization from the common people, whom the Founding Fathers certainly feared. The belief that growing popular power posed a threat to freedom and enlightenment was common among Continental European liberals in the late nineteenth century, and was to some extent shared even by the radical John Stuart Mill. More recently, fear of the undiluted power of the people was strongly reinforced in Europe by the experience of mass support for Nazism. The conviction that liberal principles need to be defended against the people marked many of the institutional structures reestablished in Europe after the Second World War, from German electoral arrangements to the European Court of Human Rights and the institutions of the European Union.

To many observers of New Populism it seems axiomatic that populism and liberalism are natural enemies (Taggart 2000, 116; Mény and Surel 2000). And despite the confusing case of Pim Fortuyn, the gay Dutch populist mentioned earlier, it is true that contemporary appeals for the return of power to the people are frequently linked with exclusive communal visions of the people that clash with liberal principles of human rights. In the longer view, however, the case is rather different. For much of its history liberalism was explicitly the cause of the people, mobilizing the excluded in the name not only of popular sovereignty but of freedom and the rights of man. We saw in chapter 2 how many-sided that cause had become by the time of the American and French Revolutions. In and through those revolutions, the cause of the people became a project that included a comprehensive set of radical demands: government that belonged to the sovereign people (not to kings or aristocrats) but also rights for the people as individuals; self-determination for oppressed national peoples but also solidarity with people in general, all humanity. The liberal side of modern democracy is deeply indebted to that multifaceted radicalism, which regularly mobilized the excluded people behind liberal and progressive causes. Both the British Liberal Party and French Republican Radicalism were populist in this sense, while representatives of the tradition in American politics were legion. Anglophone political discourse (in which 'the people' means individuals as well as a collectivity, and 'people' refers to human beings as such) makes it particularly easy for populism and liberalism to share common ground.

It is true that liberalism as an ideological project does harbour an internal tension that can set off a populist reaction, and this has a good deal of relevance to New Populism. The difficulty is one that liberalism shares with other Enlightenment ideologies of liberation and progress. In principle, these ideologies are egalitarian: *all* people are to share in liberation and enlightenment. But because those goals are to be achieved progressively, some groups are always farther ahead than others; more enlightened, more liberated, more able to show the way to the laggards. Despite its mission to all people, liberalism's belief in progress cannot avoid devaluing the existing culture, values and way of life of most of the people to whom it is addressed.

The history of the Left shows that members of the excluded people have often been willing to accept that sort of tutelage, either out of deference to their betters or because they had enough faith in progress to accept wrenching changes to their own way of life. But that acceptance cannot be taken for granted. As a consciously progressive ideology, liberalism has always had the potential to set off populist reactions against the enlightened vanguard and in defence of the dignity of the people in their unenlightened state. In the USA, acceptance of change by a mobile population has been balanced by a marked lack of deference toward intellectuals, particularly where popular religion and morality are concerned (Hofstadter 1964). Tennessee's celebrated 'Monkey Trial' in 1925, which pitted Darwinian science against popular biblical fundamentalism, foreshadowed contemporary controversies over issues on which 'progressive' opinion is at odds with grass roots convictions (Canovan 1981). One reason for expecting to see more of this anti-progressive populism is that the balance of authority between the liberal vanguard and the lagging grass roots has shifted, in Europe as well as in traditionally egalitarian societies like the USA or Australia. By the end of the twentieth century there had been a noticeable decrease in popular deference toward all authorities, while belief in progress and the march of enlightenment had weakened even among liberal elites. Some American intellectuals associated with the journal *Telos* have even advocated a new populist order in which ordinary people will no longer be expected to defer to the 'New Class' of liberal intellectuals in deciding how to live their lives (*Telos* 1991).

Clashes between New Populists and contemporary liberals over 'political correctness' tend to involve constitutional constraints as well, notably legal commitments and procedures that protect the rights of unpopular minorities such as criminals, gays and asylum-seekers. Like liberal principles, the commitment to due process of law is often thought of as an element in modern democracy that is intrinsically incompatible with 'power to the people'. But that diagnosis takes too simple a view of the relation between constitutional constraints and the will of the sovereign people. Arrangements that secure to all citizens the equal protection of the laws are in principle not hindrances to the power of the people but one of its most fundamental conditions. Defence of individual rights and due process of law against arbitrary rule by the powerful was historically one of the main elements in the people's cause, pressed for example by the Levellers and by early nineteenth-century English populists. And while impatience with some of the rambling byways of the law is certainly one element in contemporary populism, another is anger that citizens' rights of person and property are not being effectively guarded against criminal attack.

I have suggested that despite its plausibility, the two-strand analysis of the relation between populism and democracy tends to underplay the ties between liberal constitutionalism and the cause of the people. In the remainder of this chapter I shall argue that it also tends to divert analytical attention from important issues raised by New Populism. Its fear that liberal institutions and values are threatened by popular sovereignty seems to concede the dubious populist claim that 'power to the people' is a simple, straightforward programme; that it is obvious who and what the sovereign people is/are, how it/they can take action, and why such action is authoritative. My principal quarrel with the two-strand theory is, in other words, that it evades the most fundamental intellectual challenge posed by populist movements within established democracies, the challenge to think seriously about the sovereign people.

Contrary to some populist claims and many anti-populist fears, 'power to the people' cannot be cashed out as rule by opinion poll. Although populists seek to mobilize the excluded people – a supposed 'silent majority' of 'ordinary people' – they do so in the name of the people as a whole, the collective sovereign people that is commonly believed to be the ultimate source of political legitimacy. And that sovereign people is an elusive entity, not to be equated simply with a majority vote at a particular time. Indeed, 'the people' as an entity or group capable of exercising power is/are not readily available. Far from being a given, it/they has/have to be in some way constructed, mobilized or represented to be in a position either to wield power or to be checked in doing so. The people as the population of individual citizens of a state do not in themselves add up to a collective agent, and under normal circumstances constitutional rules and procedures are required to turn them into anything approximating to one (Holmes 1995: 163–9). Furthermore, we shall see in chapter 5 that no procedures, however carefully constructed, can guarantee an outcome that can be plausibly regarded as the act of the sovereign people, nor can lack of such procedures preclude the occasional appearance on the public stage of an informal mobilization that may be plausibly so regarded.

The people as sovereign authority – that mysterious being that haunts all modern politics, though it is invoked particularly stridently by populists – is not easily captured within institutional forms. A clue to some of its peculiarities can be found in the characteristic mood and style of populist movements. Although such movements may owe much of their support to the specific grievances they address, there seems often to be another aspect to their appeal. Analysts have often commented on their overheated atmosphere, on the charisma surrounding their leaders, on their lack of interest in pragmatic institutional solutions and their promise of a new beginning in politics (e.g. Taggart 2000: 99). In keeping with their stress on spontaneity rather than institutions, populist movements tend to be spasmodic, flaring up briefly and dying away almost as fast.

These features suggest that to understand New Populism we need to be aware of an important tension in modern democracy between what I have elsewhere described as 'pragmatic' and 'redemptive' styles of politics[5](Canovan 1999). From a pragmatic point of view, corresponding to the ordinary, everyday diversity of people-as-population, modern democracy is a complex set of institutions that allow us to coexist with other people and their divergent interests with as little coercion as possible. But democracy is also the repository of one of the redemptive visions (characteristic of modernity) that promise salvation through politics. The promised saviour is 'the people', a mysterious collectivity somehow composed of us, ordinary people, and yet capable of transfiguration into an authoritative entity that can make dramatic and redeeming political appearances. Although we expect to be able to translate the people's sovereignty into the practices of mundane politics, we cannot help being haunted by expectations of the political renewal that the transcendent sovereign people should somehow bring. And because mundane arrangements for political participation by ordinary people rarely enable us to *see* the people in action, modern democracy has a hole at its centre, a stage on which we can imagine that special people appearing to make a new start (Lefort 1986). The easiest way to fill that empty place – a route often taken by populist movements – is to project our hopes on to a leader who can seem to embody the people (Mény and Surel 2000: 127). But even the most charismatic of popular leaders tends to disappoint, leaving us with an unsatisfied craving for an authentic appearance by that special, redeeming people that is somehow always in reserve.

Populist movements mobilize the excluded people-as-part (whether 'common people' or 'ordinary people') by summoning up the authority of the people-as-whole. Their tense relationship with modern democratic politics has a number of causes, some of them well-aired. But one source from which populist enthusiasm comes welling up deserves more thorough exploration than it has so far received. It is the region of shadowy obscurities surrounding the fundamental conviction that contemporary populists share with mainstream political culture – the conviction that the ultimate source of legitimate power is the sovereign people. The next two chapters will attempt to shed some light on those obscurities. In chapter 6 we shall pursue the sovereign people into the realms of political myth. First, though, let us consider how much sense we can make of the notion in more conventional terms.

5

We the Sovereign People

There is one thing more powerful than the Constitution . . .
That's the will of the people. What is a Constitution anyway?
They're the products of the people, the people are the first
source of power, and the people can abolish a Constitution if
they want to.

George Wallace in Lipset and Raab 1971

In the last two chapters we have encountered some of the political complexities of popular sovereignty, looking first at the boundaries that define a people, then at populist mobilization of the people-as-excluded-part in the name of the people-as-sovereign-whole. So far we have not tried to come to grips with the fundamental notion of popular sovereignty itself. We cannot avoid doing so, however, for that notion is far from clear. It is in fact ambiguous in two overlapping ways. By long-standing tradition (as we saw in chapter 2) the sovereign people has been understood both as an abstract authority in reserve and as a concrete power to be seen in action, if only in exceptional circumstances such as revolutions. Furthermore, that people has been conceived (particularly within Anglo-American traditions) both as an immortal collective body and as a population of separate mortal individuals. The problem of popular sovereignty is therefore the attribution of ultimate political authority to a 'people' that manages somehow to be both a set of concrete individuals, taking action in a particular

place at a particular time, *and* an abstract collective entity with
a life beyond such limitations. These ambiguities are problematic both in theory and in practice. It is hard to make theoretical sense of the notion, while translating it into practical,
operational terms is even harder. When we observe particular
individual people doing things, are we ever in a position to say
that what we see is action by the sovereign people? Crucially,
can we say of any institutional practice – the election of representatives, for instance, or voting in a referendum – that its
outcome must be regarded as the act of the sovereign people?

These are the issues the present chapter seeks to address. It
may be wise to start, however, by anticipating an objection to
the way in which I have defined the problem. Some critics
would say that I am creating unnecessary difficulties by con-
flating two conceptions of popular sovereignty that are really
quite separate, each of which is relatively straightforward
within its own context. According to that view, popular sovereignty in modern states is not to be confused with legal
sovereignty. Legal sovereignty is a practical matter of laying
down the law, so that popular sovereignty understood in that
context means direct law-making by an assembled people, as
in the ancient Roman and Athenian assemblies. *Constituent*
sovereignty is quite different, being an ultimate source of
authority in reserve behind the ordinary business of law-
making and government. Popular sovereignty as it is taken for
granted in modern politics belongs entirely to this latter category. This theory has been lucidly formulated by Bernard
Yack, whose account is worth closer examination.

Yack maintains that the sovereign people that has final
legitimate authority in modern polities is a purely abstract
conception. It is understood as 'a collective body', 'the whole
body of a territory's legal inhabitants' (Yack 2001: 519),
which does not rule or legislate but delegates authority to
those who do. Stressing that he is not talking about a social
fact but about a legitimating abstraction, Yack claims that this
abstract people is universally available in modern politics,
everywhere from China to Canada, always the same and existing 'in a kind of eternal present' (Yack 2001: 521). Drawing
on the work of Edmund Morgan and Istvan Hont (Morgan
1988; Hont 1994) he maintains that this notion of the people
as constituent sovereign is a specifically modern conception

that was spread by the English, American and French revolutions and is now universal. His own interest is chiefly in the links between popular sovereignty and nationalism, discussed in chapter 3.

Yack's vivid account leaves out a number of complications. For one thing, the notion of the people as abstract ultimate sovereign is not as distinctively modern as he suggests; as we have seen, it emerged stage by stage from the Roman legacy. More crucially, although his account of the constituent sovereign people may fit French traditions (Hont 1994; Mény and Surel 2000), it cannot accommodate the complexities of Anglo-American experience. As we saw in chapter 2, that tradition does indeed contain the notion of an abstract collective people as constituent sovereign in reserve, but this is complicated by two extra features. In the first place, the sovereign people is conceived not only as a legitimating abstraction but as a body that is able (on occasion) to intervene concretely in politics and take action. In other words, while this sovereign people is clearly not a practical body exercising legal sovereignty like the Roman *populus* or the Athenian *demos*, it cannot be pushed entirely into limbo as a legitimating abstraction.

Secondly, the sovereign people of Anglo-American tradition are not just an abstract collectivity but are also concrete individuals. This is a matter of crucial importance, although it hugely complicates the tasks of conceptualizing and implementing popular sovereignty. The conjunction of unity and plurality within the tradition is striking, creating an impression that the sovereign people is *us* here and now as well as being a powerful, immortal, authoritative body of which we are members.

Although these complexities are most apparent within the Anglophone tradition, I suspect that they are not confined to it. Once the notion of popular sovereignty is available in politics it is hard to avoid attempts to translate the abstract constituent sovereignty of the collective people into political action by concrete individuals, whether in populist attempts to 'give politics back to the people' or in the constitutional referendums that have become an increasingly familiar feature of modern democracy (cf. Yack 2001: 529). The problems explored in this chapter may therefore have wider relevance, and the discussion will take in Rousseau as well as Locke.

It may be that the only way to deal with these incoherencies is to analyse the discourse of popular sovereignty in terms of what Edmund Morgan calls 'fictions' (Morgan 1988) – either the devices of ideological manipulation or the myths left behind by times of popular mobilization. We shall revisit these questions in chapter 6; meanwhile, the present chapter will try to answer two connected questions arising out of our tangled political inheritance:

1   *Can popular sovereignty be understood?*
    Can we make theoretical sense of a sovereign people that seems to be collective *and* individual, absent *and* present?
2   *Can popular sovereignty be exercised?*
    Supposing that it is possible to get a clear grasp of what popular sovereignty means, what bearing does that have on the institutions of modern representative democracy?

To anticipate the argument to be developed below, I shall suggest that a satisfactory answer to Question 1 implies a rather unsatisfactory answer to Question 2, and that while it may be possible to conceive of popular sovereignty in a way that accommodates the ambivalences of body/individuals and absence/presence, the solution that emerges is one that cannot be satisfactorily built into democratic institutions. Our first task, however, is to examine the conundrum of a sovereign people that is supposed to be both a single body and a collection of individuals, absent in abstraction but sometimes present in action. At the centre of this conundrum is the thorny question of what (if anything) it means to talk of the people as a 'body'.

1   Can Popular Sovereignty be Understood?

The Body of the People

No one within the Anglophone tradition needs to be reminded that 'the people' means concrete individuals; it is the people as a collective body that is problematic. This collective people has figured largely within the tradition, turning up in the utterances of the most determined individualists; we shall see later that 'the body of the people' has a prominent role within the theory of John Locke. But recent political theorists have paid little attention to the notion, tending to take for granted that collective conceptions of the people are the exclusive preserve of 'Continental' theories in which the people as individuals disappear into the *peuple* or *Volk* (Holden 1993: 84). That instinctive suspicion of collectivism (now reinforced by the adoption into political theory of rational choice theories from economics) is itself a warning that no theoretical articulation of a collective sovereign people can be satisfactory unless it also preserves a recognition of people as separate, plural, concrete individuals. Bearing that in mind, let us turn to possible ways of thinking about the people as a whole.

The people's collectivity has traditionally been expressed through metaphors, usually without much reflection on their implications. It is piquant that an attack on political metaphor should have been launched by one of the great populists of the American and French Revolutions, Tom Paine. There is a revealing passage in the *Rights of Man* in which he jeers at the notion that sovereignty could belong to the *Crown*. Talking about the sovereign right to declare war, he says,

> In England the right is said to reside in a *metaphor*, shown at the tower for sixpence or a shilling apiece; so are the lions; and it would be a step nearer to reason to say it resided in them, for any inanimate metaphor is no more than a hat or a cap. (Paine 1989: 86)

Paine's rejection of monarchist mumbo-jumbo is attractive, and it is easy to contrast the real flesh and blood people with that sort of metaphorical nonsense. But the real flesh and blood people cannot possess or exercise sovereignty unless they are somehow united into an entity more coherent than a collection of mortal individuals. Theorists of monarchy had adopted the metaphor of the Crown to stabilize a power and authority that fluctuated because kings, too, were mortal individuals (Kantorowicz 1957). Paine evidently did not notice that the sovereign body of the people might be as metaphorical as the Crown – though it may be significant that he himself tends to sidestep the problem by talking about the sovereign '*nation*' rather than the 'people', just as the French *Declaration of Rights* had done in reclaiming sovereignty from the king (Hont 1994: 194).

English political discourse has often fallen back on the geographical metaphor of 'the country', a term closely linked to the nation. But the most familiar image is the organic metaphor of the people as a *body* with *members*, a way of talking about social collectivities so familiar that we rarely notice the metaphor when we use it. What does it mean, though, to talk about the sovereign people as a 'body'?

The mysteries of the body of the people are most easily approached indirectly, by observing how one of the people's many incarnations has appeared to hostile outsiders. Within a long tradition of discourse running back via Horace to Plato, the *common* people were seen as a mythical beast, the 'many-headed monster'. A remarkable collection of references to this beast in seventeenth-century England, put together by Christopher Hill, betrays fear of the collective power of the common people when they act together but also provides a picture of the sort of collectivity they form (Hill 1974). The many-headed monster is a dangerous beast, full of brute force, monstrous precisely because it is many-headed and has no guiding mind. It has enough unity to be effective in destruction but it cannot reason or take responsibility.

This hostile caricature brings into focus a paradoxical feature of the image of the sovereign people as a body. The metaphor seems on the face of it to imply that, like any ordinary body, the people needs a single head. Theological images of the church as the mystical body of Christ, of which Christ himself is the head, did much to bring bodily metaphors for the realm and for the people into common use during the Middle Ages, at the same time reinforcing the monarchical connotations of the metaphor itself. Sir John Fortescue spelled out the implications in the fifteenth century:

> a people does not deserve to be called a body whilst it is acephalous, that is, without a head . . . So a people that wills to erect itself into a kingdom or any other body politic must always set up one man for the government of all that body . . . Just as in this way the physical body grows out of the embryo, regulated by one head, so the kingdom issues from the people,

and exists as a body mystical, governed by one man as head.
(Fortescue 1997: 20)

The image of the people as a body directed by a kingly
head might suit a supporter of constitutional monarchy like
Fortescue, but was less appropriate once king and people were
at odds with one another. As we saw in chapter 2, it was
through confrontations of that kind that the sovereignty of the
people in reserve was developed. If the people were to hold the
king to account, they needed to form a body that could act
independently of him, but how could they do so if he was their
head? One device tried by Parliamentarians at the beginning
of the English Civil War was to use the theologico-political
doctrine of the king's 'two bodies' (personal and official) to
claim that although the king's person might be mobilizing
troops against them at Oxford, his *regal* body was present
with them in Parliament (Morgan 1988: 55; Kantorowicz
1957: 21). But the bodily metaphor could easily be used on
the Royalist side. Thomas Hobbes used it graphically in
Leviathan (not least on the title page) to imply that it is in and
through subordination to their royal head that individual
people become members of a body politic. For though 'multitude' may be 'a collective word', it does not denote a collective entity that can take action (Hobbes 1983: 92). Only their
sovereign representative can convert them from an aggregate
of individuals into cells in the body of Leviathan. 'A multitude
of men, are made *one* person, when they are by one man, or
one person, represented . . . For it is the *unity* of the representer, not the *unity* of the represented, that maketh the person
one' (Hobbes 1960: 107). Without that sovereign representative, the people have no unified existence that could allow
them to challenge his authority. In a parallel move to the parliamentary attempt to capture the king's metaphorical body,
Hobbes claimed that despite the appearance of monarchy, the
people already *were* ruling themselves through their sovereign
representative:

> It's a great hindrance to Civill Government, especially
> Monarchicall, that men distinguish not enough between a
> *People* and a *Multitude*. The *People* is somewhat that is *one*,
> having *one will*, and to whom one action may be attributed;

> none of these can properly be said of a Multitude. The *People*
> rules in all Governments, for even in *Monarchies* the *People*
> Commands; for the *People* wills by the will of *one man* . . . in
> a *Monarchy*, the Subjects are the *Multitude*, and (however it
> seeme a Paradox) the King is the *People*. (Hobbes 1983: 151)

At first sight, then, the bodily metaphor of popular unity
might seem too closely linked with royal headship to be able
to express popular as opposed to royal sovereignty. But this
is by no means the end of the matter. Long before Hobbes
turned the image to his own monarchical ends, corporate
metaphors of the people had been used for republican and
antimonarchical purposes to articulate collective popular
power. Within that republican tradition of corporation theory,
a people organized for political action was an entirely different matter from a many-headed multitude. Even in the days of
the Roman Republic, recognized procedures had existed that
enabled the multitude in the Forum to transform themselves
for action into something much more united and dignified, the
populus Romanus. When the traditions of Roman Republicanism were revived in the medieval Italian cities, republican
jurists used metaphor to argue that the ruling people of the
city formed a body that could take action without a unifying
monarch. The fourteenth-century jurist Baldus portrayed the
city as a corporate *populus* that was more than an aggregate
of individuals, for those individuals formed a '*corpus mys-
ticum*'. Such a body might be mystical, abstract, and comprehensible only by the intellect, as Baldus said, but it was quite
capable of taking action because, like any body, it had a structure and appropriate organs. When the corporate people were
gathered in their assembly, the individuals present could themselves act as organs of the whole (Canning 1980: 13–14);
alternatively the whole body could be represented by an
elected governing council (Canning 1988: 475). The ruling
people of a republic therefore formed a *universitas* like the
many other ecclesiastical and secular corporations that were
able to exercise rights and accept responsibilities. The virtue
of understanding the people in this way was its practical
clarity. As in the case of other such legal entities, a clear distinction was made between the corporate people and a mere
aggregate of individuals. It was clear how the body of the

people was constituted, who were its members and who had authority to speak and act for it.

That version of corporation theory was intended to apply to direct popular government by the small citizen bodies of medieval city-states. But the principle of legal incorporation as a way of combining individuals into a body that can take collective action may seem to be much the same regardless of scale or setting. Modern societies play host to corporate bodies of all kinds (universities among them), each of them composed of individuals but nevertheless able to act as one, survive changes in membership, and have interests, rights and responsibilities of its own. The precise ontological status of these bodies has never been clear and has given rise to fierce juristic disputes: are they 'real' or merely 'fictitious'? Are they created only by legal fiat or do they have an existence prior to legal recognition (Hallis 1930; Gierke 1950)? But despite such uncertainties, corporate bodies evidently manage to function effectively within a framework of legal specifications, even in today's individualistic society. Why, then, should the notion of a corporate *people* be any more problematic? Could we not extend to the people of a modern nation-state the corporate analysis that Baldus applied to his city *populus*?

As soon as we ask the question, however, we can see that the sovereign people of Anglophone democracy is not that sort of body. Even if we ignore the problem of legal circularity (can corporate bodies that are defined by law include the body that is supposed to be the ultimate source of law?), clear definition is precisely what the people lacks. The Anglo-American tradition drew on notions that differed from Baldus' republican *populus*, being on the one hand more nebulous and on the other hand more concrete. Within that tradition the vast and vague image of the sovereign people in reserve was somehow linked to Anglo-American individualism. As conceived in the political struggles of seventeenth- and eighteenth-century England and America, the sovereign people is several different things at the same time. It is a numinous sovereign collectivity in reserve, extending over generations but without precise boundaries or structure; it is (at any rate on occasion) an active collectivity that can intervene in politics in defiance of king or Parliament; it is also specific flesh-and-blood individuals, the free-born Englishmen for whom Colonel Rainborough spoke at Putney (Sharp 1998: 103–15). This conglomerate notion of the people presents two connected challenges to the would-be analyst. How can the people be understood as a collective entity that simultaneously *remains* a set of individuals? And how can the people be so constituted that it can take political action while at the same time retaining its ultimate sovereignty in reserve?

One can express this dual conundrum in a rather different way. To be understood as sovereign, the people seems to need a continuing existence that transcends the birth and death of its individual members; furthermore, if it is to be sovereign it needs some form of representation to act for the whole and take decisions binding on individual members, including future generations. All this seems to imply the kind of corporate existence that Baldus had in mind, in which (as the unavoidable use of the singular in the last couple of sentences shows) individual members disappear into the whole body. But this is only one side of the story. Although the people need to be able to take collective action and therefore need to be able to generate collective representation, they and their sovereignty still remain in reserve; and despite their membership of a continuing body, they still remain the people as individuals, 'we, the people' of each specific generation.

Logically it may seem that this circle cannot be squared, and that if the notion of the collective people were ever to be coherently conceptualized, this could be done only by means of corporation theory. Either the people are simply an aggregate of individuals with no capacity for collective sovereignty and political action, or else they form a corporate body that can exist and act as other corporate bodies do. In the latter case, they are 'the people' *only* as members of the whole, not as individuals; there is no way in which they *as* 'the people' can hang on either to their individuality or to their reserve authority. As 'the people', the individuals are subsumed within the corporate whole, and the whole including the individuals is subsumed within the acts of the representatives of the whole.

And yet, inescapable as these arguments may seem, they are at odds with political experience. The conundrum with which we are faced is that the imagined sovereign people as it emerged momentously in the Anglophone tradition stubbornly continued to be collective *and* individual, present *and* in reserve. The challenge is therefore to find a way of grasping theoretically what happened politically. I shall suggest in the next section that (at any rate on one reading) John Locke attempted to do this in the *Second Treatise* that he wrote in defence of popular revolution, and that it was this effort to come to grips with political realities that made his theory less coherent than more orthodox formulations of social contract theory.

Locke and the Body of the People

By the time Locke's *Second Treatise* was published in 1690, the notion that government was founded upon some sort of original social contract was widely accepted by many political theorists across Europe. Within the tradition of Natural Law theory, the long-standing assumption that legitimate authority originated from the people had been gradually developed into a conventional discourse according to which free and equal individuals in a state of nature were supposed to have contracted to form themselves into a people which then set up a government (Gough 1936). The versions of contract theory that are widely read today, those by Hobbes, Locke and Rousseau, were idiosyncratic creations contrasting with a background tradition of more orthodox theories, elaborated over two centuries by writers in many European countries (Gough 1936; Derathé 1950). Although readers of Locke tend to associate contract theory with the liberal concern for individual rights, this is misleading. A striking feature of the tradition as a whole is that theories apparently founded upon the natural autonomy of individuals very commonly led to the authorization of an absolute monarch, and even more regularly to the surrender of individual freedom to the community as a body (Gough 1936; Tuck 1979). Hobbes was unusual in making submission to the sovereign an individual affair. According to the more usual pattern, negotiations with a monarch were supposed to follow some sort of 'compact of association' whereby individuals in an imagined state of nature formed themselves into a people, which Suarez described as a mystical body with a single will (Gough 1936: 67; Skinner 1978: 165). The clearest and most influential of these formulations was developed by the German jurist Samuel Pufendorf in his widely circulated *De Jure Naturae et Gentium* of 1672.[1] Pufendorf envisages free, abstract individuals in an original state of nature contracting together to form themselves into a body that thereby becomes a new 'moral entity', a 'compound moral person' with its own will in which the wills of all individuals are subsumed. This body then decides on the type of state to be set up, leading to a third and final phase in which the corporate people submit themselves to the rule of a sovereign – normally a monarch, possibly a council or assembly, but in all cases the repository of undivided sovereignty[2] (Pufendorf 1717: 8, 468, 497; Dufour, 1991).

Like many other European jurists, Pufendorf used the theme of contract to legitimize a strong state rather than to justify the active exercise of popular power. All the same, for English Whigs faced with a tyrannical king this notion of a corporate people might at first sight seem useful. It does after all provide an answer to Hobbes's claim that nothing but the sovereign monarch unites individuals and holds society together. On Hobbesian principles there is no collective people that can take united action to challenge the king, so that any weakening of royal authority is liable to plunge society back into the war of all against all. On the face of it, the notion of an original social compact before the establishment of government is precisely the reassurance needed that even if the government collapses, the corporate people still remains as a collective body that can act in a coherent way to restore or remake the political regime. This was in effect the view put forward by George Lawson in *Politica sacra et civilis*, often seen as an influence on Locke (Franklin 1978). According to Lawson, ultimate sovereignty lay with the people considered as a single corporate body – also, significantly, considered in national terms as 'the community of England'. When civil war dissolved the government, sovereignty returned to the people, who remained unified in their allegiance to that national body (Lawson 1992: 227–36; Tierney 1982: 97–100).

John Locke also wanted to argue that when government breaks down, a people with the right and capacity to take political action still remains. But Locke's theory is less clear and more interesting because he seems determined to maintain two apparently contradictory views of the people. Not content with conceiving of the sovereign people as a single body able to hold the king to account and to reconstitute government, Locke simultaneously understands that sovereign people as concrete individuals in full possession of their natural rights. Within more orthodox theories, as we have seen, individual autonomy disappears at an early stage, subsumed in collective choice by the corporate people. But Locke insists on the freedom of people as individuals while at the same time continuing to use the notion of the people as a body.

Describing the original social contract, Locke tells us that men in a state of nature 'enter into Society to make one People, one Body Politick' (Locke 1964: 343) and that within that single body, 'the majority have a Right to act and conclude the rest' (Locke 1964: 349). So far this seems orthodox enough. Much of his justification of revolution is concerned with the relations between this sovereign 'body of the people' and the king to whom it has entrusted power. Despite occasional suggestions that crises of the regime may cause the body itself to fall apart in the Hobbesian manner (424, 429), Locke's usual position seems to be that the people as a body survives any such crisis and is in a position to reclaim its authority and remake government (385, 424; cf. Franklin 1978). But where is this collective 'people' to be found? Not in Parliament; although on one occasion he describes that as the 'Soul that gives Form, Life and Unity to the Commonwealth' (425) he makes clear elsewhere that Parliament should not be mistaken for the people and that the powers to tax and to legislate are only lent, not handed over (380). Above all, 'there remains still *in the People a Supream Power* to remove or *alter the Legislative*' (385: Locke's emphasis) if it betrays its trust.

The most interesting feature of Locke's account is the nature of this 'people' that can act to reclaim authority from King and Parliament. For this is no abstract people, lost, like Pufendorf's, in the mists of time; Locke is clearly talking about imminent and drastic political action. It is evidently in some sense a body, that 'Body of the People' that is the only judge of when revolution is justified (426). But it is certainly not a constituted body of the legally corporate kind, and it seems in fact to be a body of individuals. Locke says that when government has broken its trust, individuals are freed from subjection and 'everyone is at the disposure of his own will'

(426); and yet he evidently expects that the individuals concerned will be able to act *as* a body, in circumstances where formal ties between them no longer exist. Earlier he had maintained that the majority must speak and act for the body of the people, but there is no attempt to operationalize this provision within his theory of revolution, nor would any such attempt have been realistic. It seems possible, as Richard Ashcraft has argued, that what he had in mind was an informal mobilization of individuals, commanding such a strong groundswell of support that it was clearly recognizable as the people – the sort of movement that actually happened in England in 1688 when James II had managed to unite almost all parties against him. According to Ashcraft, Locke was talking about a 'movement', 'a moral community rather than a distinctly organized expression of political power' (Ashcraft 1986: 310; cf. Marshall 1994: 276).

Locke's theory is notorious for its ambiguities, and there is much dispute among scholars about his intentions and the extent of his radicalism (e.g. Wootton 1993). It may be doubted whether we should go all the way with Ashcraft's picture of him as a full-blown revolutionary writing the manifesto of a socially radical movement. Like most people of his time and later, he surely took for granted that the people would find their natural leaders in the landed classes. Nevertheless, there can be no doubt that he was much closer than most political philosophers to the experience of revolutionary political mobilization. It may be that the account of popular revolution given in the *Second Treatise* makes better sense politically than it does theoretically. Despite the abstract juristic apparatus of social contract and corporate body, perhaps what Locke is interested in is popular mobilization for political action, which can reconcile individual and collective and unite absence and presence. In normal times the authority of an abstract collective people is in reserve, but in the moment of revolution (not something to which people are easily provoked) a mobilized people can emerge out of that background on to the public stage; a contingent movement of free individuals, but of individuals acting together as a body to generate power and exercise sovereignty.

This is a conjectural reading of Locke that may not seem persuasive to scholars. It is offered here simply as the beginning of an answer to the wider problem posed at the start of this chapter: the problem of how the apparently contradictory conceptions of the sovereign people so firmly entrenched in the Anglophone tradition might be understood. The suggestion being made here is that although the various facets of the sovereign people cannot be reconciled in juristic terms, they may on occasion make practical sense in moments of political action, as was perhaps the case in 1688–9. They may be briefly reconciled, that is to say, by the appearance on the public stage of a mobilized body of individuals who are able (in the particular circumstances of that time and place) to present themselves as the people with enough credibility to generate power and authority. However, this tentative answer to the question of how to *understand* the sovereign people makes even more pressing the second question posed at the start of this chapter: can popular sovereignty be *exercised* in the context of modern democracy?

2   Can Popular Sovereignty be Exercised?

Locke's sovereign people might be capable of revolutionary action, but they were rising to restore limited monarchy, not to institute democracy and exercise power themselves. Nevertheless, if the notion of a sovereign people can make sense on occasions of popular mobilization, it is natural to ask whether the exercise of popular sovereignty might not be possible on a more regular and continuous basis. In this section I shall consider that question from three angles, looking first at the relation between the people and their representatives; secondly at 'direct democracy', or the notion that referendums can make the exercise of popular sovereignty a regular feature of modern democracy, and finally at the quest for some sort of general will of the sovereign people, whether in Rousseau's original version or (in more recent theories) to be achieved through public deliberation.

The People and their Representatives

Radical Whigs might see the Glorious Revolution as a manifestation of the sovereign people in action, an occasion when the free people of England asserted their ultimate authority and acted as a body to change the regime. But the gap between revolutionary eruption and constitutional practice was underlined in the following century by the entrenchment of the doctrine that it was *Parliament* that was sovereign: the prime principle of English constitutional law was that the King-in-Parliament alone can actually exercise sovereignty (Goldsworthy 1999: 181–8). No doubt (English jurists conceded) the people were the ultimate source from which King, Lords and Commons drew their authority; in cases of dire emergency direct popular action might even be necessary, as it had been in 1688, but that was not something that could be catered for in constitutional law. In any case, long-standing constitutional tradition held that when King, Lords and Commons were assembled, every member of the people was also present and consenting to what was done, so that acts of Parliament *were* acts of the people. The first statute passed by James I's Parliament in the early seventeenth century had summed up that tradition by declaring that Parliament was a High Court 'where all the whole body of the realm, and every particular member thereof, either in person or by representation . . . are by the laws of this realm deemed to be personally present' (Goldsworthy 1999: 96; cf. Reid 1989: 12–14; Pitkin 1967: 246). In this characteristic formulation, the apparently opposed attributes of the people are united: though absent, they are deemed to be present, and they are a single body though composed of distinct persons.

The union of these conflicting themes within English tradition nevertheless imposed strains on the notion of representation, as Parliament found in the mid-eighteenth century when it tried to tax the American colonies. Events in America challenged not only these specific powers but the whole notion of parliamentary sovereignty. A mobilized American people 'appealed to heaven' and rose in revolt as Locke had recommended; they then went further, asserting their sovereignty through the adoption in popular conventions of written constitutions. Jeffrey Goldsworthy observes that this 'gave concrete, practical form to the previously abstract, theoretical idea that the power of an elected legislature ultimately belonged to the people it represented, who alone were truly sovereign' (Goldsworthy 1999: 209). 'We the People of the

United States' were proclaimed authors of the Federal Constitution, while the new republican political system was explicitly designed as a form of 'popular government'. Since the establishment of the USA, popular sovereignty has apparently been institutionalized. Even in Britain, where the sovereignty of Parliament continued to be a constitutional dogma, increasing accountability to a universal electorate enhanced Parliament's role as the voice of the people, making it possible (up to a point) 'to reconcile . . . the legal sovereignty of Parliament and the political sovereignty of the people' (Goldsworthy 1999: 219).

As we saw in chapter 2, however, the new kind of popular government established by the Constitution of the United States was strangely ambiguous. There could be no doubt that it was to be *the people's* government: that was demanded by radicals and conceded by the Federalists. But its distinctive feature, marking it off from the popular governments of antiquity, was that it was representative government. The people were to be absent from the people's government. This curious duality of presence and absence, which continues to be characteristic of modern democracy, has been most lucidly analysed by Bernard Manin. Manin distinguishes modern representative government from two alternatives, direct popular self-government on the one hand and what he calls 'absolute representation' on the other. Direct popular self-government, as in the classical republican model, leaves no room for a gap between governing people and governed. At the opposite extreme, 'absolute representation', most trenchantly formulated by Hobbes, implies, in Manin's words, that 'the people acquire political agency and capability of self-expression only through the person of the representative. Once authorized, however, the representative entirely replaces the representer. They have no other voice than his.' But Manin argues that this Hobbesian theory does not accurately depict modern representative government, 'in which the representatives can never say with complete confidence and certainty, "We the people"'. As he says, representative government as we know it leaves open a 'gap' between governors and governed, so that despite being represented, the people remain outside and sometimes 'reveal themselves as a political entity capable of speaking apart from those who govern' (Manin 1997: 174; cf. Pitkin 1967).

It seems, then, that we still need an account of the sovereign people of modern representative democracy as distinct from the representatives it/they periodically elects/elect: as an absent authority in reserve, but capable also of making its presence felt. Two opposed accounts are available, one of which leans toward an individualist understanding of the people, the other toward a more collectivist conception. According to the first, the people can exercise their sovereignty directly by means of referendums; according to the second, a collective popular will can be arrived at by processes of deliberation. As a way of making the sovereign people present, each has its own problems; along both routes, however, there is a gulf between *occasional* appearances of what may be plausibly regarded as the sovereign people, and the regular institutionalization that the notion of active sovereignty seems to demand.

Let the People Decide! Referendums and Popular Sovereignty

Asked to say what the exercise of popular sovereignty means, many citizens of modern democracies would point to referendums and the other practices that are usually summed up under the heading of 'direct democracy'. And when circumstances call for some momentous decision concerning the future of the country – secession or merger, major constitutional change – we find it natural to say that 'the people' should decide, and mean by that a decision by the majority of us, the voters. Populist agitators are not alone in assuming that the outcome of such a vote can be taken to be a decision by the sovereign people. The purpose of this section is to consider whether or not that assumption is plausible.

Referendums come in as many different shapes and forms as elections, and not all of them are democratic. In Europe, use of manipulated plebiscites by dictators from Napoleon to Hitler gave direct voting a bad name in many quarters until late in the twentieth century. In recent decades, however, referendums on constitutional issues have become increasingly common, and interest in other forms of direct democracy has been spreading, heightened by the new technological scope for voting on line (Budge 1996). The USA has a long history of direct voting. Although there is no constitutional provision for a nationwide referendum, some states (notably California) are accustomed to the use of the citizens' initiative, whereby a proposition for legislation can be put on the ballot paper by any organisation that can collect enough signatures. The undisputed homeland of direct democracy is Switzerland, whose citizens are continually asked to vote on new laws or on constitutional changes proposed by citizens' initiatives (Butler and Ranney 1994; Magleby 1984; Kobach 1993).

Our concern here is not with the pros and cons of direct democracy but with a more limited question: is the practice of direct democracy equivalent to action by the sovereign people? This equation is widely assumed and may seem obvious (Bogdanor 1994: 24). In Switzerland, announcements of the outcome of the latest round of popular voting take the form, 'the Sovereign of Switzerland has accepted (or rejected) the following propositions . . .' (Linder 1994: 91). Note, however, that this latter illustration is not quite as straightforward as it may seem, as we can see if we recall the distinction mentioned earlier between legal sovereignty on the one hand and the 'constituent' sovereignty of the people on the other. *Legal* sovereignty is a matter of having a procedure for settling disputes, by providing an authoritative verdict that cannot be overridden elsewhere. In a modern democracy, that last word may be declared by a popular vote, as in Switzerland (Kobach 1993: 41), but it may alternatively come from an act of the Queen in Parliament, as traditionally in Britain, or from the Constitution as interpreted by the Supreme Court, as in the USA.

From an institutional point of view, that is, referendums and initiatives belong to the toolkit of devices used within various liberal democracies in order to conduct political affairs in an orderly manner. Like other procedures, they have advantages and disadvantages, and these can be considered without much reference to the notion of action by the sovereign people; most academic discussion of direct democracy is in fact conducted in these pragmatic and procedural terms (e.g. Saward 1998). It is questionable whether the notion of the sovereign people can be entirely excluded from such discussions. Nevertheless it is quite clear that (contrary to populist and common sense assumptions) there is no necessary equivalence between the authoritative outcome of a referendum and a verdict by the sovereign people.

Why not? What *would* be involved in a verdict by the people? As we have seen, the notion of the sovereign people is doubly ambiguous. It means the people as concrete individuals here and now, but also the continuing collective body of which they are members. To say that the outcome of a referendum is a verdict by the sovereign people is to claim that something more has happened than simply the recording of individual votes. The claim is that the continuing, collective and usually absent people has made its presence felt in the votes of the concrete individual people; that in the majority decision[3] those votes combine to deliver the choice of the whole people, binding not only on the losers but on future members of the people. We cannot simply assume that any and every referendum can be described in these terms. On the contrary; to describe a referendum as an act of choice by the sovereign people is a great deal more plausible in some circumstances than in others. As we shall see, this has two implications. On the one hand, the very fact that we can distinguish degrees of plausibility shows that the notion of action by the sovereign people is not meaningless. On the other hand, the institutions of direct democracy cannot be relied upon to deliver such action.

On what grounds can we distinguish between more and less plausible claims that the result of a particular referendum is equivalent to a decision by the sovereign people? What are the relevant factors? These questions are most easily approached negatively, by specifying circumstances that reduce the plausibility of such claims. The most obvious concern boundaries and collective identity.

1   *Are the electorate a people?* Although the borders of polities have been delivered by historical contingencies, politicians and theorists usually find it convenient to take them for granted and assume that they contain a political community – a people. But this is not necessarily so, and in some cases it is very obviously not so. Such cases amount to a powerful argument that democratic politics needs a collective people, by showing what can happen where there is not one but two peoples, one of which does not accept the existing borders of

the polity. A referendum held in such circumstances cannot be expected to deliver the verdict of *the* people and to provide an authoritative solution. A classic case is the 1973 border poll in Northern Ireland. Faced with conflict there between Protestant Unionists (loyal to the United Kingdom) and Catholic Nationalists (who had never accepted the partition of Ireland that left the North out of the independent Irish Republic) the British government tried to resolve the issue by handing the decision to 'the people of Northern Ireland'. The result of the referendum was a resounding 98.9 per cent in favour of remaining within the United Kingdom, a verdict hailed by Unionists as a clear expression of the will of the sovereign people. It cannot be doubted that this was the will of the *Unionist* people, a collective body of considerable strength and durability. But the misleading landslide was the result of mass abstention by the minority Catholic *Nationalist* people. Knowing that they would be outvoted, and challenging the validity of the poll because the boundaries of polity and electorate cut across their own people, they expressed their own collective will by staying away (Butler and Ranney 1978: 212).

Boundary issues perhaps offer the most striking evidence of circumstances that can lower the plausibility of regarding a referendum result as a decision by the sovereign people. But many other circumstances are relevant, including the following.

2 *Intimidation, corruption and manipulation*: Even a unanimous decision on a 99 per cent turnout lacks plausibility if the voters have been coerced or bribed into voting. And even without such blatant distortions, powerful interests may be able to skew the result of a referendum and then present it as evidence of backing by the sovereign people. Where a referendum is organized by a government for its own purposes, at its chosen time and on a question framed to suit its interests, there may be grounds for suspicion if it goes the way it was designed to go (though this is by no means a foregone conclusion in modern democracies). Even citizen initiatives outside official control cannot necessarily be regarded as pure emanations of grass roots democracy. Direct democracy in California has generated a flourishing initiative industry, providing those who have the necessary funds with professional collection of signatures and expertise in framing propositions and campaigning for them. David Magleby's researches into

the effects of this found that although the lavish spending of money could not guarantee positive success for an initiative, negative effects were much easier to bring about: money spent trying to defeat an initiative was cost-effective (Magleby 1984: 147; cf. Kobach 1993: 241–3). Evidence of successful manipulation by any of these means will make us doubt whether the people really have spoken.

3   *Popular apathy or confusion*: James Fishkin mentions one referendum (a local one, Dallas, in 1978) in which only 2.1 per cent of the registered electorate bothered to take part (Fishkin 1991: 58). Even the most dedicated of populists would find it hard to hear the voice of the people in a whisper as feeble as that, so that the level of turnout is a relevant consideration. Evidence that many of those who vote do not know what they are voting about would have similar implications. Propositions are sometimes confusingly framed, obliging voters to vote 'No' to signal positive support for a law, and there is evidence of voters inadvertently casting their votes the wrong way as a result (Magleby 1984: 141–4).

4   *Mixed messages*: In recent decades, students of democracy have devoted a great deal of ingenuity to the paradoxes of voting as revealed by theorists of rational choice. These paradoxes arise when individual choices are put together to generate a collective decision. Each voter's preferences among the available alternatives may be quite rational and coherent, but in combination they yield arbitrary and incoherent results. William Riker famously used choice theory to attack 'populism', or the doctrine that the point of voting in elections is to discover and declare the will of the people (Riker 1982: xviii). Riker's claim has been subjected to a great deal of sophisticated and technical discussion (summarized in Budge 1996; Weale 1999). In contrast to the elections with which he was concerned, referendums are less vulnerable to this kind of attack because they characteristically restrict the voter's choice to two options, making the connection between individual choice and collective outcome transparent (Riker 1982: 59–60; Budge 1996: 148). But incoherencies of a rather different kind can emerge from a series of referendums or initiatives that produce results inconsistent with one another, for example sanctioning an expensive policy but voting down the tax required to pay for it.

Mixed messages of another sort can emerge from a single vote. There have been many cases in which a hard-fought campaign on some sensitive issue has led to widespread popular interest in and awareness of the issues at stake and a high turnout of voters, but where the resulting majority was too slim to be regarded as a conclusive result. If the people have spoken, they did so with a forked tongue. Even more ambiguous are the numerous cases where many people seem to have paid little attention to the topic at issue but seized the opportunity to punish the government (Franklin et al. 1995). It may of course be argued that the negative vote itself amounts to an authentic judgement by the people, but even that cannot be taken for granted. One of the regular features of Swiss direct democracy is the '*neinsager*' vote, a disposition on the part of a significant proportion of citizens to vote indiscrimately against any proposal that is put in front of them (Kobach 1993: 88; cf. Butler and Ranney 1994: 172).

To sum up, whatever the merits of direct democracy as a set of convenient decision-making procedures, there are many reasons for caution in treating its outcomes as decisions by the sovereign people. But the implications of this are more interesting and less negative than might at first sight seem to be the case. The very fact that we have grounds for ruling out that interpretation of referendums in many cases shows that we can discriminate between more and less plausible cases: in other words, we seem to know what an authentic verdict of the people would be like. Reversing the negative factors that we have examined, we can say in summary that claims to hear the voice of the sovereign people have maximum plausibility in the following circumstances: where an electorate with a strong sense of forming a political community[4] takes part in a free and uncorrupt vote on a topic that is widely understood and has high salience for the general public. The wording of the proposition is clear and free of bias, the turnout is high and the majority is overwhelming. These conditions cannot be met without an unusual degree of public discussion and political mobilization, so that individual voters are aware of taking part as members of the people in a shared choice. A referendum of this kind is a notable political event that confers legitimacy on its outcome, and it seems reasonable to agree that on the rare occasions when something like this occurs (usually in votes concerned with national independence)[5] (Butler and Ranney 1978: 8) we can speak of the sovereign people being present and taking action.

When this happens, however, it is due not so much to the referendum procedure as to the popular mobilization that has taken form around it. Although a collective people may sometimes be made manifest through the votes of individual people, no procedure can guarantee this. The referendum and initiative can of course be defended on pragmatic grounds (Budge 1996), but the populist claim that putting issues to the electorate is equivalent to giving politics back to the sovereign people fails, and we must be clear *why* it fails. The problem is not (as Riker would have it) that the whole notion of the sovereign people is meaningless, nor (as Yack maintains) that it has meaning only as an abstraction. The truth is messier and more complicated than either of these claims. For it seems on the one hand that the collective people can on occasion be more than an abstraction and may appear as a powerful political phenomenon. On the other hand, it seems that while procedures such as referendums may provide convenient channels through which such occasional bursts of political energy can flow, they cannot be counted on to capture and institutionalize the voice of the people.

Looking for the sovereign people in the practices of 'direct democracy', we have found that it is not entirely absent but is decidedly elusive; we have found, furthermore, that where it is present, this is in the context of a mobilized public in which individuals have become engaged. There seem to be affinities here with a style of thinking about the people and collective choice quite different from the individualist and proceduralist approach we have been exploring, namely the idealist tradition stemming from Rousseau. This has recently been revitalized in the form of 'deliberative democracy' and the next section will consider whether we can best understand the sovereign people within its terms.

Let the People Talk! Popular Sovereignty and Deliberation

The trouble with referendums, according to James Fishkin, is that they amount to decisions by 'a people who are not a public' (Fishkin 1995: 23) whereas the task of democracy is 'to bring power to the people under conditions where the people can think about the power they exercise' (Fishkin 1991: 1). His own solution is what he calls a 'deliberative opinion poll' in which a representative sample of voters gather to discuss an issue in circumstances where information is available to them, and conclude their discussion by voting. In contrast to ordinary opinion polls, Fishkin claims that an exercise of this kind has legitimacy because it reveals what the people *would* think if all of them had this opportunity for informed discussion (Fishkin 1991: 81). It is easy to hear echoes in this of Rousseau's contrast between the will of all and the general will. This is not surprising, for although contemporary discussions of deliberative democracy differ in important ways from Rousseau's theory, his spirit haunts the literature. Starting from his position may therefore help to clarify the issues at stake.

Rousseau's theory of popular sovereignty is complex and many-sided. Although his legacy has been associated with Jacobin collectivism (and even with 'totalitarian democracy') (Talmon 1952) he was heir to the tradition of social contract theory (Derathé 1950) and was much concerned with the problem of uniting individual and collective aspects of the people; furthermore, he had a republican aspiration to make the abstract sovereign people present in politics. Within his theory reconciliation is achieved by means of a *volonté générale* that is directed to the common good and is ideally just, but that is also willed by the people (both as individuals and as a body directly assembled). But although in principle the general will should unite an ideally rational solution to the problems of political life with the will of a collective people, Rousseau doubted whether the people themselves would be able to bring about this feat of reconciliation (Rousseau 1987: 162). A lawgiver is therefore conjured up, enlightened enough to see what the general will is and charismatic enough to form individual citizens into a cohesive people that can be counted on to will it. He must, says Rousseau, be able 'to transform each individual (who by himself is a perfect and solitary whole) into a part of a larger whole' (Rousseau 1987: 163).

Contemporary theories of deliberative democracy may in some ways be seen as updated versions of Rousseau's theory, with the crucial difference that the lawgiver has disappeared from the picture (or at any rate retreated into the shadows). The two jobs that Rousseau expected him to do – achieving an enlightened resolution of conflicting interests and forming a popular consensus behind it – still need to be done, but the people are now expected to do both jobs themselves by means of deliberation. The large and highly sophisticated literature on deliberative democracy that has appeared in the past couple of decades contains different strands, some of them more concerned with the issue of enlightened decision-making than with the matter of achieving a collective popular will, an aspiration that some theorists consider misconceived (e.g. Knight and Johnson 1994: 284). It is often assumed, however, that one of the purposes of deliberative democracy is to make manifest the will of the sovereign people (e.g. Bohman and Rehg 1997: ix) and that the practice of deliberation can itself accomplish something analogous to Rousseau's transformation of individuals into parts of the citizen body. Coming to the discussion with our individual views and interests, we find that others have their own perspectives and that in order to persuade them we must appeal to general interests and principles, experiencing in the process what David Miller calls 'the moralizing effect of public discussion' (Miller 1993: 83; cf. Cohen 1997: 77; Warren 2002: 183, 186).

Sustained participation in public deliberation should according to this theory develop a sense among those involved of belonging to a political community engaged in a common enterprise (Miller 1993: 83; Cohen 1998: 222; Barber 1984: 133–52). Like Rousseau, deliberative democrats recognize that the consensus at which deliberation ideally aims is unlikely to produce unanimity, leaving a role for voting. As in Rousseau's theory, however, the majority verdict that completes the deliberative process is taken to be more than an arbitrary aggregation of conflicting individual wills, and to count as evidence of the strength of the majority's arguments (Manin 1987: 359; Cohen 1997: 75; Rousseau 1987: 206). In this 'formation of the collective will' (Manin 1987: 355) or of 'joint intentions' (Richardson 1997: 377) optimists hope to find genuine self-determination by an enlightened collective people.

How realistic is this hope? For present purposes we can leave aside the issue of enlightenment; we are concerned here not with the pros and cons of deliberative democracy in general (see Bohman and Rehg 1997; Elster 1998) but with the more specific question whether or not deliberative processes can be plausibly supposed to reveal a sovereign people in action. Compared with our discussion of referendums there is an extra difficulty here, in that it is hard to say what counts as an example of the practice of deliberation. For some of its advocates, deliberative democracy is a radical ideal that would be quite different from the liberal democratic politics we are familiar with (Dryzek 2000; Barber 1984). Others, notably Habermas, take it to be something that is already more or less present in the practice of western democracies.

Within Habermas's theory, the notion of popular sovereignty makes a fleeting appearance, only to disappear again into the complex procedures of liberal democratic politics. In an essay reflecting on the legacy of the French Revolution, Habermas explicitly repudiates the collectivist conception of popular sovereignty that was part of that legacy:

> The people from whom all governmental authority is supposed to derive does not comprise a subject with will and consciousness. It only appears in the plural, and *as* a people it is capable of neither decision nor action as a whole. (Habermas 1996b: 469)

In this context and elsewhere Habermas rejects any 'embodiment' of the sovereign people as a 'self' or 'subject' with a 'will', sounding strikingly individualistic as he speaks of a '*decentered* society' making 'the success of deliberative politics depend not on a collectively acting citizenry but on the institutionalization of the corresponding procedures and conditions of communication' (Habermas 1994: 7). Interestingly, he denies any intention 'to denounce the intuition connected with the idea of popular sovereignty' and the 'communicatively generated power' it involves. But his version of popular sovereignty is disembodied and dispersed throughout the complex public institutions, procedures, practices and discourses that contribute to the working of a modern democratic polity (Habermas 1994: 10; 1996: 486). Compared with Bernard Yack's conception of the people as a legitimating abstraction it is nevertheless relatively substantial, for

Habermas's 'proceduralized' version is tied to the mechanisms that make it possible for individuals and groups to contribute to the formation of public opinion, policy and law-making. What it rules out is anything actually recognizable as the people in action, what Frank Michelman calls 'the ongoing social project of authorship of a country's fundamental laws by the country's people, in some nonfictively attributable sense' (Michelman 1997: 147).

That stronger conception of popular sovereignty has a particular appeal for radical deliberative democrats. In Benjamin Barber's influential account of 'strong democracy', the point of deliberation is to form a common will on the basis of which citizens can act collectively to change the world. Seeking to cross the gulf between theory and practice, Barber added proposals for a whole battery of participatory institutions that would complement representation and turn individuals into active members of a political community (Barber 1984). Unlike the abstract discussions offered by many deliberative democrats, these concrete proposals (which include neighbourhood assemblies meeting once a week) allow us to see quite clearly why deliberative democracy is no more reliable than referendum democracy as a way of making the sovereign people present. The reason is obvious: offering individuals the *opportunity* to become part of a deliberative community cannot in itself induce them to attend weekly meetings and participate in the right spirit, nor to feel themselves part of a common endeavour. The missing link, in deliberative as in 'direct' democracy, is the collective mobilization that alone can make the people present, but that happens rarely, if at all. This may be further cause for scepticism about the notion of an active sovereign people. But there is one theorist, Bruce Ackerman, who has made a serious effort to take on board both the customary absence of any such people and evidence of its occasional presence.

In his study *We the People* Ackerman is concerned with American experience, specifically with the interaction between constitutional continuity and the occasional crises when system change has emerged out of exceptional popular mobilization. He characterises the spirit of the US Constitution as 'dualist democracy'. During long periods of 'normal politics', decisions are made for the people by their elected government within the framework of the Constitution. But he maintains that there are periods of 'higher law-making' that significantly alter the Constitution, during which it really can be said that 'the People' deliver a decisive verdict (Ackerman 1991: 6, 266; 1998: 5). Such occasions are rare, for most people most of the time are not deeply engaged with politics (Ackerman 1991: 299; 1998: 6). Once in a while, however, in response to some issue or crisis, a movement for change builds up such depth and breadth of support that its claim to be the voice of the People becomes convincing. In such a 'constitutional moment' the weight of mobilization is such that 'there is a broad sense, shared (bitterly) by many opponents, *that the People have spoken*' (my emphasis, Ackerman 1998: 409; 1991: 272).

According to Ackerman there have so far been three of these 'constitutional moments' in the history of the USA: the original adoption of the US Constitution; Reconstruction after the Civil War, and the New Deal in the 1930s. One of his aims in writing is to propose a new institutional structure that would facilitate and channel further movements of the sort, shifting the emphasis in constitutional change away from Supreme Court judges and back to the people. His scheme includes both deliberation and direct popular voting, and is meant to supplement representative government. He stresses that his proposed procedure would be much more demanding and serious than a quick referendum reflecting a fleeting public mood. To be regarded as authentic, a movement must be able to survive a lengthy period of 'mobilized deliberation' (Ackerman 1991: 285; 1998: 4) and the procedure he proposes would allow plenty of time for initiatives to run out of steam if they did not gain really serious popular backing. But his proposals are intended to vindicate his belief that 'in America, the People rule' (Ackerman 1998: 92) – at any rate on the rare occasions when they choose as a body to do so.

Ackerman's theory is unusually concrete, being concerned with America and its special circumstance, and the historical interpretations on which it hinges are inevitably contentious. Pervading his work is a vivid sense of the USA as a 'national community' (Ackerman 1991: 36) and it is clear that this greatly reinforces his conviction that there *is* such a thing as an American People, even though it is normally in reserve. Curiously, although the term 'People' is capitalized throughout (with plural verbs), it is not until nearly halfway through

Volume II that he stops to explain what he means by it. Denying that he has in mind any conception of the People as 'a superhuman being' able to 'speak' as an individual, he tells us that he has been speaking metaphorically, but that 'For me, "the People" is . . . the name of an extended process of inter-action between political elites and ordinary citizens' during which ordinary Americans are drawn out of their private lives into 'the project of citizenship' (Ackerman 1998: 187).

Assessment of Ackerman's success or failure in the ambitious task he has set himself is beyond the scope of this book. Regardless of that verdict, however, his approach is relevant to the present argument because it highlights the occasional and spasmodic nature of the sovereign people as well as the power and authority that its eruptions can generate. It also recognizes and tries to cater (in the very special circumstances of the USA) for the uneasy relationship between this elusive people and the institutions of modern representative government.

Conclusion

The riddle of popular sovereignty is that despite the power and authority it conveys, the notion is beset with contradictions that are especially glaring within the Anglophone political tradition. The sovereign people are/is at one and the same time a collection of mortal individuals and a lasting collective body; furthermore, although this body is normally absent from the political stage, dwelling in reserve in the realms of abstraction, it is also capable of making its presence felt in powerful and authoritative political action. Faced with these problems, this chapter addressed two questions:

1 Can popular sovereignty be understood? Can the notion be analysed in terms that are clear and yet do justice to its contradictory features?
2 Can popular sovereignty actually be exercised, especially in the context of modern representative democracy?

I suggested earlier that success in answering question (1) would spell problems in addressing question (2), and we are now in a position to see why this is so. I have argued that if we are to understand popular sovereignty and make sense of its apparent contradictions, we need to think of the sovereign people not simply as a timeless abstraction but as an outcome of political mobilization. What we are dealing with is not just an 'imagined community' (Anderson 1983) but an occasional community of action: the rare appearance on the public stage of a large-scale movement in which individuals are consciously united as the people and act as a collective body. What we are concerned with, in other words, is more than an idea and is (at times), something that happens (cf. Brubaker 1996: 18) or is thought to happen. Classic examples of such events perhaps occurred in England in 1688/9, in America during the Revolution and (within living memory) in Poland at the height of the Solidarity movement of the 1980s (Touraine et al. 1983). Examples within the context of liberal democratic institutions might include those cited by Ackerman, or the occasional cases of decisive referendums on matters of great political moment. In the clearest cases such mobilizations generate power and authority, leaving behind the memory – or myth – of the sovereign people in action.

From a constitutional point of view this sovereign people is profoundly unsatisfactory. It is occasional and unpredictable. It is never comprehensive enough to include all potential members, and its status as the *real* people is always more or less contestable. It is not the sort of entity that can actually rule or that can be institutionalized as a sovereign in the legal sense. Modern democratic institutions are nevertheless both sustained and overshadowed by the idea and the myth of the sovereign people. That mythic aspect is the subject of the next chapter.

6
Myths of the Sovereign People

'*Wir sind das Volk*'[1]

The last chapter concluded that despite its theoretical contradictions, the notion of the sovereign people can perhaps make
sense in political practice – but only in those rare cases of successful mobilization where a collection of individual people
turns into a body that can take collective action, briefly con-
verting the idea of an absent people into something that is
present and powerful. I also suggested, however, that to
appreciate the notion's political force we need to pay attention
to myths as well as to events. Of all 'the people's' ambiguities,
it may be that the most crucial is its ambivalence between the
everyday and the mythical: between the people as ordinary
members of the population, and as transfigured into a People
that has powers of political redemption. Oscillation between
the two senses is common not only in populist rhetoric but
throughout modern politics.

This claim may raise a few eyebrows. Outside the extrava-
gances of populists, does 'the people' really have such exotic
connotations in modern western politics? Asked to give an
account of the notion, most of us would take it to mean
simply the population, a conglomeration of unremarkable
human beings who happen to inhabit the territory in question.

Universal suffrage means that no special privileges or duties of citizenship distinguish the political 'people' from others, while the blurring of class divisions has made the old 'common people' (with their menace or their pathos) fade into 'ordinary people'. The term may seem to have become thoroughly demystified, in keeping with the temper of the times. But we should not be deceived. Alongside this everyday people, the western political imagination is haunted by a quite different 'People': the population transformed into a mythic being that is not only the source of political legitimacy, but can sometimes appear to redeem politics from oppression, corruption and banality.

Anyone who doubts its continuing power should reflect on the extraordinary events that heralded the collapse of Communism in Eastern Europe, and on the way they were experienced by both participants and observers. The outpouring of political enthusiasm and emotion that saturated those events, shared even by the journalists who witnessed them, took shape through the old myth of a redeeming People that can suddenly appear in politics, shake off the shackles of oppression and establish a new realm of freedom (Garton Ash 1990: 65, 77; Reich 1990: 86–7; Bakuniak and Nowak 1987: 403; Touraine et al. 1983: 5). That brief surge of collective faith and hope was hugely powerful and undeniably momentous. Once the dust has settled, of course, such intoxication may seem irrelevant to the concerns of mundane politics. Trying to damp down excessive political enthusiasm, Ralf Dahrendorf remarked in the immediate aftermath of the revolutions that 'democracy is a form of government, not a steam bath of popular feelings' (Dahrendorf 1990: 10). Nonetheless, in a world where the ideology of popular sovereignty is prevalent, the significance of that exhilarating moment of faith in the People can hardly be ignored.

In counterpoint to the banal ordinariness of the-people-as-population, then, we need to take seriously the hectic career of the People as myth. The significance of myth within the politics of nationalism is widely recognized (e.g. Schöpflin 1997), and I shall argue that myths of the people (some of them overlapping with nationalist myths) (Smith 2003) deserve just as much attention. The first part of this chapter considers myths set in the past and in the future, their links with events and their interpretation in the present. The second section tries to confront some difficult questions about these phenomena. To what extent can we treat such myths simply as manipulative fictions, empty devices to be unmasked? Should we perhaps see them as pointers to something more authentic, even as encapsulating hidden truths about political power and authority?

1   Myths of the People

In his book *Political Myth*, Henry Tudor argues that 'myth' is a complex phenomenon not to be confused with mere deception. Three of the features he points to are particularly worth stressing here: a political myth as he understands it has dramatic form; it concerns a political collectivity of some kind, and it has a practical political point. As the collective story of a state, a nation, or some other political group it is neither pure fiction nor straightforward history, but it is invoked because it makes sense of political experience. In particular, it allows individuals to identify themselves with 'our' collective story and provides them with patterns of behaviour. It is practical in the sense that it either legitimizes existing political conditions or justifies political action: any particular myth can be told in many different ways and adapted to many different practical circumstances (Tudor 1972).

Tudor does not explicitly discuss myths of the sovereign people, but much of his analysis is relevant here, notably his distinction between stories about the past and about the future. Backward-looking myths of the sovereign people include foundation myths about the popular origin and authority of polities (cf. Smith 2003). These can be subdivided into local and universal foundation myths, though there has been a good deal of interaction between the two; the local kind tells a quasi-historical story about the popular origins of a particular polity, whereas the universal kind is some version of the story of the social contract, according to which all legitimate polities are founded on popular consent.

Local foundation myths tell the story of how a particular people in a particular time and place rose against tyranny, and established their own polity on the basis of popular sovereignty. The most venerable version still in circulation is the

Swiss foundation myth, which tells how the peasants of the original cantons (among them William Tell) defied their feudal oppressors and met on the Rütli meadow to swear mutual assistance, thereby founding a popular, self-governing federation. Another local myth that has had more widespread echoes is the French Republican foundation myth of the great Revolution, especially the storming of the Bastille by the people. This myth was given classic form in the nineteenth century by the historian Jules Michelet, who made a point of insisting that the only real actor in the dramatic events of the French Revolution was the People as a whole (Michelet 1967: x, xiii, 12, 162). But in terms of influence in contemporary politics, the most significant of all backward-looking local myths of the people is the foundation myth of the United States of America. That story (which is interwoven with the religious myth of a divinely chosen people) starts with the Pilgrim Fathers fleeing persecution and founding their polity on the Mayflower Covenant, and goes on to tell how the American people rose against George III, won their War of Independence and established their own Constitution by their own authority, 'We, the People of the United States . . .'. Each of these myths legitimizes a particular polity, and also provides grounds where necessary for recalling that polity to its foundations and giving power back to the people.

These local myths have long been thematically intertwined with the universal foundation myth of the social contract, which tells a story of how polities were founded by the people in an original state of nature. That myth is less historically-based and circumstantial, more abstract and fictional than local stories. Its heyday came in the seventeenth and eighteenth centuries, when it was told and retold in many versions with different practical messages. But although it went out of fashion during the great age of nationalist and Marxist myths, it has turned out to be quite resilient. With the revival of liberal democratic political philosophy in the late twentieth century, echoes of the myth of the original contract could once again be heard, above all in John Rawls' *Theory of Justice* (Rawls 1972). In recent versions, any lingering claims to historicity have been stripped away and both Original Position and popular consent are clearly fictitious. But the story of the popular foundation of a legitimate polity still carries persuasive force: this may not be what the people ever *did*, but it is what they would and should have done, given the chance.

As Henry Tudor shows, myths always come in a range of versions; any foundation myth can be told and retold in different ways to carry different political messages (Tudor 1972: 47, 91). Where the Original Contract is concerned this is very clearly the case. Hobbes told the story of a polity founded on popular consent, but since the most vivid part of the story as he told it was the war of all against all in the state of nature, what the myth taught was obedience to the ruler. A generation later, Locke retold the story in a way that carried the opposite political message, that the People have the right and the power to rebel in defence of their lives, liberties and properties. That, and the more or less similar versions of the story current in the eighteenth century, helped to inspire the American rebellion against Britain and the making of the American foundation myth.

It is worth pausing for a moment to reflect on the place of myths in the development of liberal democratic politics. We tend to think of the pioneers of liberalism as rationalists, men of Enlightenment; John Locke and Thomas Jefferson certainly thought of themselves in that way. But liberal democrats are no more immune to the influence of political myths than nationalists or Marxists, although they see politics within the frame of a different set of stories (Canovan 1990). Whenever the question arises of establishing a new polity and giving it legitimacy, we still turn to the myth of popular foundation, and try to re-enact it by putting the new constitution to a referendum through which the People (not just a motley collection of individuals who happen to be on the electoral roll) are supposed to speak.

These backward-looking myths of the popular foundation of polities are complemented by forward-looking myths of political renewal, to come about when the People take back their power and make a new start (cf. Billington 1980: 160; Sorel 1950). Tudor distinguishes sharply between foundation myths and myths of revolution, perhaps because his example of the latter is the Marxist myth. The peculiarity of Marxism is that the world after the revolution is to be radically new; not just a renewal of a lost past but an entirely unfamiliar kind of society inhabited by a new kind of human being. That vision bears obvious resemblances to Christian millennarianism. By contrast, revolutionary myths of the People tend to be closely tied to the past. Their central theme is the renewal and redemption of politics that will come when the People recover their lost power and freedom. There are perhaps affinities here with older monarchist myths of the sleeping hero who will one day return to save his realm: King Arthur still sleeps in Avalon. A version of the myth of popular renewal that had a long run in English radical circles was the story of the English people casting off the Norman Yoke. From the Levellers in the seventeenth century to the Chartists in the nineteenth, radicals told the story of how, in the days of Anglo-Saxon liberty, the English people had governed themselves and enjoyed their rights. The Norman Conquest had robbed them of that freedom, but the day was coming when they would rise against the relics of that conquest and reclaim their rights (Hill 1968).

This basic theme – the story of how the People have been robbed of their rightful sovereignty, but will rise up and regain it – has (as we saw in chapter 4) been the staple of populist politics for the past two centuries, particularly in the USA. Ever since the principle of popular sovereignty was officially proclaimed in the American Revolution, American populists have tried to mobilize radical action by telling some version of a story that might be summarized as follows:

> *The USA was founded by the People, as the Constitution itself proclaims. Ever since then they have been robbed and cheated of their sovereignty by politicians in the pay of 'the money power'. But the people will rise up to take back their own, in a great struggle between the forces of good and the forces of evil.*

The populist myth of redemption and renewal is a story with considerable dramatic force in its own right, but its particular strength in the United States is that it echoes the local foundation myth, allowing the two to reinforce one another.

Whether they deal with past foundation or future renewal, myths of the people are stories about the transfiguration of ordinary individual people into a powerful collective actor. If such stories linger, it is presumably because they have some relevance to the present. One of the claims made about myths

by Tudor and other commentators is that they have a unifying effect on the groups by which and about which they are
told (e.g. Schöpflin 1997: 35). Thus nations pass on their
nationhood by telling the next generation stories about their
glorious past and their struggles against their traditional
enemies; Marxist proletarians used to develop a sense of solidarity by telling one another the story of the class-struggle and
the glorious revolutionary future. But how does this apply to
the People? As we saw in the last chapter, one of the difficulties of attributing collective sovereignty to 'the people' is that
in normal times they do not apparently form a group at all.
Can the myths we have been considering be said to have a unifying effect comparable to national or proletarian myths,
unless (as quite often happens) they are fused with one or both
of the latter?

   If they do, it may be in a more complicated way, for the
myths create an expectation of popular unity that normal
experience continually disappoints. The foundation myth
according to which we, the People, are somehow the source of
political authority, gives the impression that we ought to be
able to exercise power as a body and enjoy a sense of powerful agency. But although democratic processes allow us to
have an input into politics (as individual voters, or as members
of groups of various kinds) there is rarely any clear connection between activity and effect, and certainly no sense that we
as the People are in control. As Claude Lefort says, the place
of power remains empty, or at any rate the sovereign people
remain absent from it (Lefort 1986: 279). Established democracies are indeed bad places to look for plausible appearances
by a collective People, for it is in the nature of political
freedom to encourage opposed interests and differences of
opinion to appear. Everyday politics is concerned with the
things that divide us, not the things that unite us. Citizens of
a democracy may believe half-heartedly in the myth that we,
the People, are the ultimate sovereign, but what we actually
see in the place of power reserved for the people is the squab-
bles of politicians, lobbyists and spin-doctors.

   From a functionalist point of view, the foundation myths of
the People that we in modern democracies take for granted
may be of limited use in legitimizing the existing democratic
political system. Crucially, however, they are supplemented by

faith (which seems to survive the disillusioning experience of elections) in the possibility of future renewal through the agency of the people. The effect is to leave us on the one hand with a grudging acceptance of democracy, but on the other with a craving to see the real sovereign People in action, moving into Lefort's 'empty place of power' and exerting their sovereign authority at last. This may be the reason why any plausible approximation to that scenario becomes charged with mythic power. No wonder that we willingly suspend disbelief on the rare, electrifying occasions when the myth of the People in action is convincingly enacted before our eyes (or at any rate in front of the television cameras). This is what we saw in the events that led up to the collapse of Communism in Eastern Europe, first in the rise of the Polish Solidarity movement in the early 1980s, and then in the mass demonstrations of 1989, especially in East Germany. Here, it seemed, was the foundation myth of democracy coming to life in the mundane present. Recalling some of the scenes of so-called 'People Power' that appeared on our television screens during the collapse of Communism in Eastern Europe, we might say that it is possible for the collective People to become the protagonist in a mythic drama, not just in the sense that the story can be told afterwards, but in the more immediate sense that this People seemed to make an appearance on the public stage. The mythic dimension may indeed have increased in political significance since the advent of television, which played a crucial role in 1989 in helping events to assume dramatic form and making them present to millions of viewers (Schöpflin 1997: 25).

That exhilarating sense of popular unity was doomed to disappear very rapidly. The people who were throwing off Communist rule were not really about to take collective control of their future and emerge into a redeemed world: the very best they could expect would be mundane democratic politics of the kind practised in the states of the European Union. Politically, however, what mattered was that the myth of the People in action was so widely believed: believed by the participants themselves, like the demonstrators in Leipzig who baited the rulers of their 'People's Republic' by chanting '*Wir sind das Volk*'; believed by western journalists and television audiences; even believed by the collapsing

Communist governments. These events were *moving*, not just in the sense of inspiring emotion on the part of observers, but in the practical sense of setting people in motion. In acting out the myth of popular sovereignty, the participants were able to make it come true to the extent that they did mobilize individuals, thereby generating popular power and bestowing popular sanction on the new polities.

Brief as they were, those stirring events left two enduring legacies. One was the tangible political effect of popular mobilization, its contribution to the fall of Communism and the establishment of new democratic polities. The other legacy was a set of new myths of popular action and foundation. The democratic republics in question now have their local foundation myths, but the wider legacy has been to reinforce the universal democratic myths of people power, popular foundation and popular renewal.

I have been arguing in this section that if we are to understand the politics of 'the people' we need to pay some attention to the myths that can legitimize authority and set people in motion, generating 'people power' to destroy and create regimes. Apart from recognizing the political efficacy of such myths and enactments, how should we regard them? Are they 'mythical' in the sense of being untruths, delusions or deceptions? Crucially, is their collective hero, the People, itself a myth?

2   The People as a Fiction

Inventing the People is the title of a study by Edmund Morgan, one of the few scholars who has paid close attention to the sovereign people. Despite protesting that his 'purpose is not to debunk' (Morgan 1988, 15) he repeatedly speaks of the sovereign people as a 'fiction' that was deliberately invented and used by political elites for their own purposes, originally to challenge a similar fiction, the divine right of kings. According to Morgan, the decisive role in the creation of this fiction was played by English Parliamentarians in the course of their opposition to Charles I. In order to liberate themselves not only from the King, but also from their own constituents, 'representatives invented the sovereignty of the people in order to claim it for themselves. . . . In the name of *the* people they became all-powerful in government' (Morgan 1988: 49–50).

Morgan goes on to trace the use of this fiction by its supposed representatives during the American Revolution, and he makes clear that what he considers 'fictional' about it is the very notion of a collective sovereign people, not just the annexation by representatives of that people's power. Indeed he suggests that this notion is actually further from reality than the vision of a monarch by divine right.

> A king, however dubious his divinity might seem, did not have to be imagined. He was a visible presence, wearing his crown and carrying his scepter. The people, on the other hand, are never visible as such. Before we ascribe sovereignty to the people we have to imagine that there is such a thing, something we personify as though it were a single body, capable of thinking, of acting, of making decisions and carrying them out . . . (Morgan 1988: 153)

Morgan's analysis sharpens the issues that need to be addressed, for calling the People a 'fiction' may have one or more of four different implications.

- 'Fiction' suggests deliberate invention by a particular agent or agents at a particular time and place – by English Parliamentarians in the 1640s, according to Morgan.
- 'The sovereign people' and any supposed appearance or collective action by them may be fiction as opposed to reality, perhaps on the grounds (implied by Morgan) that only individuals can be real.
- 'Fiction' may refer to deception for political purposes, where rulers use an imaginary 'people' to induce a belief in their legitimacy.
- Calling the sovereign people a 'fiction' may imply that any action, consent or legitimation attributed to that fictitious people is a sham, so that regimes relying on it are not really legitimate at all.

Although these four steps form a logical progression, they do not stand or fall together. Despite his sceptical manner, Morgan himself is reluctant to take the final step and conclude that the political legitimacy allegedly derived from the sovereign people is a sham (Morgan 1988: 14–15). He also wobbles on Step 2 ('fiction' versus 'reality'), at times almost conceding that in some circumstances (particularly in the American colonies at the time of the Revolution) a collective sovereign people might not be entirely fictitious after all (Morgan 1988: 90, 122, 137, 237). Most of the points he wants to make might be less contentiously expressed in the language of 'myth', which permits a more nuanced treatment, though without allowing us to evade the sceptical points raised above. One respect in which 'myth' is clearly preferable to 'fiction' in referring to the sovereign people is that the former suggests a product of collective imagination over time rather than a deliberate and specific invention. Morgan's talk of the 'invention' of the sovereign people in mid-seventeenth century England is inaccurate, for while he is right to point out the new uses to which the notion was put, these would have been much less effective in the absence of a familiar story about power coming originally from 'the people'.[2] But even if we think of this imagined sovereign people as myth rather than fiction, we are still left with the other questions raised by his sceptical account:

• If the sovereign people is/are a myth, does that mean it/they cannot really exist or act?
• Is the myth of the sovereign people simply a manipulative device used by its supposed representatives to deceive those they control?
• Can a mythic People confer genuine political legitimacy?

3   The People as Myth and Political Reality

One of Morgan's grounds for scepticism seems to be an assumption (common in the Anglophone world) that only individuals *can* be real, so that an imagined collectivity must be unreal. We saw in chapter 5 that the ontological status of social collectivities is a good deal more complex than that, with many of them reaching a high level of institutional solidity. That earlier discussion nevertheless concluded that 'the sovereign people' is too elusive to be entirely captured by any such institutionalized collectivity. It may help if we approach those elusive features by means of a theoretical framework more subtle than Morgan's methodological individualism. The sociologist Pierre Bourdieu has interesting things to say about the imagined collectivities that furnish the world we experience, and particularly about the importance of 'naming', which can conjure into existence the group it seems to describe.

In many respects Bourdieu's approach to these collectivities is as sceptical as Morgan's. Where Morgan spoke of 'fiction', Bourdieu uses the language of magic and sorcery to describe the processes by which collectivities are generated and 'symbolic power' wielded in society. Seemingly academic arguments about identities, classifications and the boundaries of groups may in fact be 'struggles over the monopoly of the power to make people see and believe, to get them to know and recognise, to impose the legitimate definition of the divisions of the social world and, thereby, to *make and unmake groups*'(Bourdieu 1991: 221). When people do come to see themselves and others in terms of such group identities, the groups in question become part of the social world. But as Bourdieu observes, 'It is easy to understand why one of the elementary forms of political power should have consisted, in many anarchic societies, in the almost magical power of *naming* and bringing into existence by virtue of naming' (Bourdieu 1991: 236).

Since human beings understand their world in symbolic terms and act accordingly, a collectivity that has been conjured up by this magical process and become part of common sense perception is evidently 'real' rather than 'fictitious' – real in the sense that anyone moving about the social world is liable to come up against it as an objective presence. But Bourdieu is nevertheless sceptical about the authenticity of activities attributed to these groups, and acutely aware of the opportunities they provide for manipulation and for the exercise of power in their name. Thinking of a wide range of collectivities, including 'the people', he speaks of 'the mystery of ministry', which 'is at its peak when the group can exist only by delegating power to a spokesperson who will bring it into existence by speaking for it, that is, on its behalf and in its place' (Bourdieu 1991: 249). When someone emerges to speak for a group and act as its representative, we tend to assume that the group must have been in existence and able to delegate authority. But Bourdieu insists (in a quasi-Hobbesian argument) that delegation is 'an act of magic' that turns a collection of individuals into a 'mystical body'; in the process, that body and its individual members lose control over the power they are generating to the representative who is supposed to be their servant (Bourdieu 1991: 209). He has some wry comments on the manipulations involved even when such groups make their appearance on the public stage. Representatives of 'the working class', for instance, can summon it up like a spirit, or 'manifest it symbolically through *demonstration*, a sort of theatrical deployment of the class-in-representation' (Bourdieu 1991: 250). In other words, although a collectivity that can appear in political demonstrations can scarcely be a 'fiction', its authenticity may be open to question.

Bourdieu shows that the practical reality of social collectivities – even, sometimes, their visible appearance on the public stage – does not dispose of questions about manipulation. In all the myths discussed earlier in this chapter, the figure of the People is a figure of authority – the ultimate political authority, in fact. If that figure can take shape only when 'conjured' or 'demonstrated' by Bourdieu's political magicians, what becomes of its authority? Before we settle for scepticism, however, we need to consider whether some appearances attributed to a mythic People may be more authentic than others, in the sense of being more spontaneous and less attributable to the dark arts of political manipulation.

The mythic People may indeed have two aspects, figuring on the one hand as a spirit summoned by political sorcerers, but on the other hand as something more spontaneous and less controllable, a movement that occasionally happens (cf. Brubaker 1996: 16). If this is so, then myths of the people appear in a rather different light, as expressions not just of the top-down symbolic power of those who make use of them, but also of the grass roots power generated by rare but memorable cases of collective action. In order to understand such occasional manifestations of 'people power' we need a dual approach that complements the investigation of more-or-less manipulative 'magic' with an analysis of movements. These occasional popular manifestations have some kinship with the episodes of collective political action known as 'social movements'. The latter are notoriously fluid, and according to one well-known study, continuity over time is made possible not by organizational form but by the persistence of collective identity after political activity has subsided. 'Movements characteristically alternate between "visible" and "latent" phases.' The collective identity in question is 'simultaneously static and dynamic', on the one hand a solid, continuous identity to be evoked, on the other something produced and continually redefined in and through collective action. It is preserved and passed on through symbols, memories, stories and ritual practices (Della Porte and Diani 1999: 85–9, 97–8).

Although that account was designed with examples like the Greens in mind, it could just as well be applied to recent cases of 'people power'. Certainly 'the sovereign people' as concept and myth is well-suited to provide a collective identity round which fluid political enthusiasm can take shape, and which can be powerfully realized in collective action. At the very least, the well-documented phenomena of social movements suggest that appearances of the people on the public stage do not have to be exercises in Bourdieu's manipulative sorcery; the possibility exists that such manifestations may be spontaneous. It does not follow, however, that any spontaneous movement claiming to be the People must be either authentic or authoritative. If it is the case (as we saw in chapter 5) that even the formal rituals of election and referendum cannot guarantee the presence of the sovereign people, the credentials of informal and fleeting eruptions must be even more open to question.

Some of the complexities of 'people power' become apparent in an account of the East German revolution of 1989 by a notable participant, Jens Reich. Reich recounts the efforts of the original handful of dissidents to make sure that their movement was representative, including 'a cross-section of normal people'. He gives a vivid description of the drama and heroism of the candlelit marches with which these ordinary, defenceless people – more and more of them as the weeks went by – ritually challenged the power of the regime. 'A myriad small, fragile points of light saying, "We are here! In our unity we are invincible because *we are the people!*"' He describes the exalted mood of the participants, impelling them to make 'magnificently foolhardy, theatrical and deeply impressive gestures' (Reich 1990: 73, 87). What becomes apparent from his account of the transfiguration of ordinary people into The People, however, is the crucial importance of the political setting in authenticating these manifestations. Against the background of the German Democratic Republic, a repressive regime that was supposed to have a monopoly of representation and mobilization of the people, any such spontaneous public action took on an exaggerated significance. Reich notes that the Communist leaders themselves were taken in by a kind of optical illusion, in that 'they overestimated the power and significance of the street protests'. Leaders in democratic regimes are much less easily persuaded that crowds in the streets really are the People. 'In the West, ruling elites have learned long ago that people come and shout, get hungry and bored after a while and return home. You simply have to "sit it out"' (Reich 1990: 86).

Of all recent cases of 'people power', the strongest claim to authenticity as a grass roots movement of the People belongs to the Polish 'Solidarity' movement that emerged unexpectedly in 1980. No sorcerer conjured or controlled those events, which seem to have been a source of astonishment even to those involved.[3] One of the most striking features of the movement was its awe-inspiring scale: in its heyday, and in the teeth of official hostility, it mobilized ten million people out of a population of less than forty million. It could do so because it represented the people three times over, not just as sovereign source of legitimacy but as underdogs and as nation – a conjunction of meanings of 'people' and sources of myth that greatly reinforced one another. Starting as a workers' trade union, it drew deeply on the rich mythology of Polish nationalism, itself fused with religious devotion. That is not to say that it had the support of the entire population, (Tymowski 1991–2: 168) but it was certainly impressive, not least in the discipline and restraint shown by such an enormous grass roots movement. To many observers this was a genuine manifestation of the People in action (see e.g. Goodwyn 1991; Laba 1991; Touraine 1983; Bakuniak and Nowak 1987). Should we then regard it as one of those moments of 'fugitive democracy' hailed by Sheldon Wolin: the fleeting revolutionary moments when, as Locke had claimed, 'power returns to "the Community" and agency to "the People"', and when 'the political is remembered and recreated' (Wolin 1994: 21, 23; cf. Goodwyn 1991: 117)? Those are the moments our political myths lead us to crave; let us now consider what conclusions we are entitled to draw from them.

Conclusion

There can be no doubt that, like all political myths, those in which the people figure offer ample opportunities for delusion and manipulation. We must nevertheless recognize that in rare cases – of which Solidarity was surely one – the appearance of a collective people cannot be dismissed as mere 'fiction' or as the smoke and mirrors of 'sorcerers'. Sometimes, it seems, we are confronted with 'the people' as a political reality, generating both the collective power that can threaten a regime, and the collective authority that can bestow legitimacy on a new one and keep that power in being (Arendt 1963). It is therefore fair to say that some of the myths contain a kernel of truth about politics: where individual people do form 'a people' and act as 'the people', political power can come into being – perhaps momentarily, but sometimes in a solid, lasting fashion, as the *populus Romanus* showed long ago, and the American People more recently. Having conceded that point, however, we need to balance it with more sceptical observations about both the power and the authority of any collective 'people'. Where power is concerned, after all, there have throughout history been cases of popular mobilization – not fictitious, not 'conjured' up – that have certainly generated collective power, but to no purpose except destruction. Fear of mob violence has been and continues to be well-founded in many settings (cf. Canovan 2002c). That reminder underlines a further question we need to ask about the mythic People: even in the rare cases where popular mobilization is neither shocking nor futile, and where it does indeed lead to a new political order crowned with popular legitimacy, how much deference is due to the authority of the collective people – 'We, the People of the United States', for instance?

There are certainly grounds for treating such a people with respect, and the principal reason should perhaps be spelled out. Citizens of western countries are too ready to take for granted the relatively civilized political conditions they enjoy, forgetting that politics in most times and places has been thoroughly predatory. Achieving a type of politics that is less predatory, and geared to some conception of the public good, is not easy under any circumstances, and may be impossible in the absence of certain preconditions. One of those preconditions seems to be a collective people, sustained by myths and capable of generating and monitoring political power (Canovan 1996). Despite all the good reasons for what Michael Oakeshott called 'the politics of scepticism', it seems that liberal democracy cannot do without a modicum of 'the politics of faith'[4](Oakeshott 1996).

Decent respect does not, however, entail uncritical deference. Loss of belief in other sources of authority – Custom, King, Church or Party – has led some to venerate the People. Nothing in the argument presented here requires that conclusion. The most potent (and most misleading) myth of all is surely the belief that somewhere, behind the mundane surface of everyday politics, there must be some ultimate source of authority that could save us from the responsibility of muddling through as best we can.

7
Conclusion

I have tried to show that the conflicting senses of 'the people' point to significant and unresolved political issues, all connected in one way or another with the attribution of ultimate political authority to the people. Chapter 2 sketched some of the ways in which those senses have persisted and mutated through a long history of controversy. Examining issues raised by the indeterminate borders of 'a people', chapter 3 explored national and anti-national conceptions of political community, and broader problems about the relation of any particular 'people' to people in general. In chapter 4, the capacity of 'the people' to mean both part and whole of the political community led us into the dynamics of populism and its uneasy relationship with modern democracy. Turning in chapter 5 to 'the sovereign people', with its deep ambiguity between a collection of concrete individuals and a collective and usually abstract entity, we encountered theoretical and practical problems that can perhaps be resolved only on rare occasions, through the temporary mobilization of individuals acting as a body. Pursuing that theme of spasmodic, uneven political activity, chapter 6 looked at the strange double life that allows the people-as-population to be transfigured into the People as redeeming presence, at any rate in the realm of myth, and at the issues concerning fiction and authenticity this raises.

'The people' is undoubtedly one of the least precise and most promiscuous of concepts. For that very reason, however, it has a claim to be regarded as a quintessentially political concept, in two respects. One of its claims to political prominence is unflattering. 'The people' is every politician's friend; its indeterminacy and ambiguities, its combination of resonance and banality make it a convenient support for all manner of causes (cf. Canovan 1984). But there is a more interesting reason for describing 'the people' as quintessentially political, which is that the concept's characteristic features mirror the contingency of politics itself. It is, as we have seen, a peculiarly open and indefinite notion (cf. Laclau 2005). Although many of its senses refer to a collectivity of some sort and can on occasion refer to a specific and defined group, the notion is characteristically amorphous, considerably more so than that notoriously elusive concept, 'nation'. 'The people' cannot be restricted to a group with definite characteristics, boundaries, structure or permanence, though it is quite capable of carrying these senses. Furthermore, its lack of spatial definition is compounded by discontinuity over time. We have seen that 'the people' often seems to refer to occasional mobilizations that appear unpredictably and fade away again.

While features like these are frustrating for political analysts looking for clear meanings and permanent structures, they are also highly characteristic of politics, and especially of the aspects of politics that are hardest to analyse. Ever since Plato, students of politics have looked for clarity and permanence behind the flux of events and appearances, seizing avidly on whatever stability they can find. Clear and precise ideas; structures such as bureaucratic hierarchies, political organizations and constitutions; regularities of voting patterns or cycles of regime change; the importance of such features is undeniable, but concentration on them does tend to divert attention from more elusive phenomena. Yet politics in general – modern democratic politics in particular – is characterised by openness and contingency; by 'events', including the rapid emergence of new initiatives and ideas, the unexpected mobilization of individuals into powerful groups, the spasmodic rise and fall of movements, and unpredictable changes of mood between enthusiasm and apathy. These features are mirrored in the openness of 'the people', which reflects the potential for commonplace individuals to come together into a political body and generate power where there was none before (Arendt 1972: 143).

In conclusion, then, the concept of 'the people' – or, to be more precise, the cluster of ideas and discourses associated with the term – may be hard to deal with, but within contemporary politics it is harder to do without. We certainly cannot afford to ignore it.

Notes

Chapter 2   'The People' and its Past

1   The same was true of *demos* in Greek (Finley 1983:1), although Aristotle identified it firmly with the mass of poor citizens (Aristotle 1992: 187, 190, 192).

2   The ambiguities between these different meanings of *populus* are clearly visible in one short passage from a speech by Cicero quoted by Fergus Millar, in which Cicero shifts easily between the inclusive, inter-generational corporate sense and that referring to the crowd of individual plebeians before him in the Forum. Translating the passage into English, Millar has to make explicit the shift between singular and plural senses (Millar 1998: 173).

3   How *much* power, compared with the senatorial class, is a matter of dispute among historians of Rome (Millar 1998).

4   See Pocock 1987: 31, on pouring new wine into old bottles.

5   Hence the five-yearly census in the Roman Republic (Lintott 1999: 115).

6   According to Sir John Fortescue, writing in the fifteenth century, the English people had enjoyed the same laws since the days of the ancient Britons. No conqueror had presumed to change them because they were so manifestly the best available (Fortescue 1997: 26).

7   Classically articulated by Colonel Rainborough during the Putney debates in 1647 (Sharp 1998: 103).

8   Filmer had a point. One chaplain in the New Model Army maintained that 'This Army are truly the *people of England,*

and have the nature and power of the *whole* in them' (Morgan 1988: 75).

9   'The government adopted here is a DEMOCRACY . . . The word DEMOCRACY is formed of two Greek words, one signifies *the people* and the other the *government* which is in the people . . . My Friends, let us never be ashamed of DEMOCRACY.' Elias Smith in 1809, quoted in Wood 1992: 232.

10 'The words "people of the United States" and "citizens" are synonymous terms . . . They are what we familiarly call the "sovereign people", and every citizen is one of this people . . . The question before us is, whether . . . [descendants of black slaves] . . . compose a portion of this people . . .? We think they are not . . .' Chief Justice Taney, quoted in Commager 1949: I 340.

11 Even Jeremy Bentham, an admirer of the USA who was normally too methodologically puritan and individualistic to deal in vague collectivities like 'the people', was provoked by government repression into using traditionally populist language in the 'Introduction' to his 'Catechism of Parliamentary Reform' (1817), Mack 1969: 320; cf. Hazlitt 1991: 12.

12 'Smile at us, pay us, pass us; but do not quite forget; For we are the people of England, that never have spoken yet' (Chesterton 1933; 173; cf. Canovan 1977).

13 Like other radicals, suffragettes appealed to the language of the people, as in a 1914 leaflet issued by the National Union of Women's Suffrage Societies: 'SHALL THE PEOPLE RULE. Asquith says No. He is trying to pose now as the PEOPLE'S champion but when millions of unenfranchised PEOPLE ask for VOTES HE is the man to flout this request . . .' (Holton 1986: 123).

Chapter 3   Ourselves and Others: People, Nation and Humanity

1   A contemporary example is perhaps the emergence of a new Palestinian people out of the struggle with Israel.

2   On myths of the people see chapter 6.

3   '*Peuple*' was considered in some quarters to be too plebeian. The implications of the sense of 'people' in which the term refers to the lower orders as distinct from the elite will be considered in the next chapter.

4   The term 'people-making' is used by Rogers Smith, (Smith 2003) but in a broader sense that includes 'nation-building' and the formation of political communities more generally.

5   Since 11 September 2001 those who wish or need to justify closure have been able to appeal to considerations of security against terrorism, an escape from the moral dilemma that has in some quarters been adopted with an audible sigh of relief.

Chapter 4   Part and Whole: People, Populism and Democracy

1   Taggart originally used this label to make comparisons with the 'new politics' of recent social movements.
2   For a contrary view see Taggart 2000.
3   The *Narodniki* are the most conspicuous example, but see for example G. K. Chesterton in early twentieth-century England (Canovan 1977), and the group around the journal *Telos* in late twentieth-century America (*Telos* 1991).
4   Anticipating current debates, a substantial body of analysis along these lines was produced in the mid-twentieth century by political scientists alarmed by McCarthyism in the USA and the memory of fascism elsewhere, only to be denounced as 'democratic elitism' when the 1960s brought an upsurge of romantic enthusiasm for grass roots participation in politics. See for example Bachrach 1967.
5   Note that this distinction does not correspond to the 'two-strand' theory of democracy criticized above. Although some liberal defenders of the theory would certainly take a pragmatic view of democratic institutions, a decidedly redemptive style of politics has been more characteristic of liberalism in general.

Chapter 5   We the Sovereign People

1   Translated into English as *Of the Law of Nature and of Nations*.
2   This abstract collective people is a direct ancestor of Yack's abstract constitutive sovereign (cf. Hont 1994).
3   In the Swiss case, a double majority of individual votes and of the cantons that make up the Swiss Federation.
4   Typically, but not necessarily, a nation, as we saw in chapter 3.
5   Though in 2002, on a turnout of 88 per cent, a referendum in Gibraltar recorded 98 per cent in favour of retaining the territory's present links with Britain.

Chapter 6   Myths of the Sovereign People

1   'We are the People', slogan of the East German demonstrators in 1989.

2   As we saw in chapter 2, variations on that myth can be traced back to the story of how the Roman *populus* handed over their power to the emperor.

3   Jacek Kuron, one of the most prominent dissident intellectuals associated with Solidarity, is said to have remarked of the events of August 1980. 'I thought it was impossible, it was impossible, and I still think it was impossible' (Tymowski 1991–2: 165).

4   As Oakeshott himself acknowledged.

References

Ackerman, B. 1991: *We the People I: Foundations*. Cambridge, Mass.: Harvard University Press.

Ackerman, B. 1998: *We the People II: Transformations*. Cambridge, Mass.: Harvard University Press.

Allcock, J. B. 1971: Populism: a brief biography. *Sociology*, 5, 371–87.

Anderson, B. 1983: *Imagined Communities: Reflections on the Origin and Spread of Nationalism*. London: Verso.

Archibugi, D. and Held, D. (eds) 1995: *Cosmopolitan Democracy: an Agenda for a New World Order*. Cambridge: Polity.

Arendt, H. 1963: *On Revolution*. London: Faber and Faber.

Arendt, H. 1970: *On Violence*. London: Allen Lane.

Arendt, H. 1972: *Crises of the Republic*. San Diego: Harcourt Brace.

Arendt, H. 1998: *The Human Condition*. Chicago: University of Chicago Press.

Aristotle. 1992: *The Politics*, ed. T. J. Saunders. London: Penguin.

Ashcraft, R. 1986: *Revolutionary Politics and Locke's Two Treatises of Government*. Princeton: Princeton University Press.

Augustine, Saint 1998: *The City of God Against the Pagans*, ed. R. W. Dyson. Cambridge: Cambridge University Press.

Bachrach, P. 1967: *The Theory of Democratic Elitism: a Critique*. Boston: Little, Brown.

Baehr, P. 1998: *Caesar and the Fading of the Roman World: a Study in Republicanism and Caesarism*. New Brunswick, NJ: Transaction.

Bagehot, W. 1872: *The English Constitution*, 2nd edn. London: Henry S. King.

Bailyn, B. 1967: *The Ideological Origins of the American Revolution*. Cambridge, Mass.: Harvard University Press.

Bakuniak, G. and Nowak, K. 1987: The creation of a collective identity in a social movement: the case of 'Solidarnosc' in Poland. *Theory and Society*, 16, 401–29.

Barber, B. 1984: *Strong Democracy: Participatory Politics for a New Age*. Berkeley: University of California Press.

Barry, B. and Goodin, R. E. (eds) 1992: *Free Movement: Ethical Issues in the Transnational Migration of People and of Money*. New York: Harvester Wheatsheaf.

Beer, S. H. 1993: *To Make a Nation: the Rediscovery of American Federalism*. Cambridge, Mass.: Harvard University Press.

Betz, H-G. 1994: *Radical Right-Wing Populism in Western Europe*. London: Macmillan.

Betz, H-G. 2002: Conditions favouring the success and failure of radical right-wing populist parties in contemporary democracies. In Y. Mény and Y. Surel (eds), *Democracies and the Populist Challenge*. Basingstoke: Palgrave, 197–213.

Biagini, E. F. 2000: *Gladstone*. London: Macmillan.

Billington, J. H. 1980: *Fire in the Minds of Men: Origins of the Revolutionary Faith*. London: Temple Smith.

Black, A. 1980: Society and the individual from the Middle Ages to Rousseau: philosophy, jurisprudence and constitutional theory. *History of Political Thought*, 1, 145–66.

Black, A. 1992: *Political Thought in Europe 1250–1450*. Cambridge: Cambridge University Press.

Blackstone, Sir W. 2001: *Commentaries on the Laws of England*, ed. W. Morrison, Vol. I. London: Cavendish.

Blau, J. L. (ed.) 1947: *Social Theories of Jacksonian Democracy: Representative Writings of the Period 1825–1850*. New York: Hafner.

Bogdanor, V. 1994: Western Europe. In D. Butler and A. Ranney (eds) *Referendums Around the World: the Growing Use of Direct Democracy*. London: Macmillan, 24–97.

Bohman, J. and Rehg, W. (eds) 1997: *Deliberative Democracy: Essays on Reason and Politics*. Cambridge, Mass.: MIT Press.

Bonwick, C. 1977: *English Radicals and the American Revolution*. Chapel Hill: University of North Carolina Press.

Boorstin, D. J. 1988: *The Americans: the National Experience*. London: Cardinal.

Bourdieu, P. 1991: *Language and Symbolic Power*. Cambridge: Polity.

Bright, J. 1868: *Speeches on Questions of Public Policy*, ed. J. E. Thorold Rogers, Vol. II. London: Macmillan.

Brubaker, R. 1996: *Nationalism Reframed: Nationhood and the National Question in the New Europe*. Cambridge: Polity.

Bryce, J. 1888: *The American Commonwealth*. London: Macmillan.

Budge, I. 1996: *The New Challenge of Direct Democracy*. Cambridge: Polity.

Burgh, J. 1971: *Political Disquisitions*, Vols I–III. New York: Da Capo Press.

Burke, E. 1834: *The Works of the Right Hon. Edmund Burke*, Vol I. London: Holdsworth and Ball.

Butler, D. and Ranney, A. (eds) 1978: *Referendums: a Comparative Study of Practice and Theory*. Washington, DC: American Enterprise Institute.

Butler, D. and Ranney, A. (eds) 1994: *Referendums Around the World: the Growing Use of Direct Democracy*. London; Macmillan.

Butterfield, H. 1949: *George III, Lord North and the People, 1779–80*. London: G. Bell and Sons.

Calhoun, C. 1982: *The Question of Class Struggle: Social Foundations of Popular Radicalism during the Industrial Revolution*. Oxford: Blackwell.

Canning, J. 1980: The corporation in the theory of the Italian jurists. *History of Political Thought*, 1, 9–32.

Canning, J. 1988: Law, sovereignty and corporation theory 1300–1450. In J. H. Burns (ed.), *The Cambridge History of Medieval Political Thought, c.350–c.1450*. Cambridge: Cambridge University Press, 454–76.

Canning, J. 1996: *A History of Medieval Political Thought 300–1450*. London: Routledge.

Canovan, M. 1977: *G. K. Chesterton: Radical Populist*. New York: Harcourt Brace Jovanovich.

Canovan, M. 1981: *Populism*. London: Junction Books.

Canovan, M. 1982: Two strategies for the study of populism. *Political Studies*, 30, 544–52.

Canovan, M. 1984: 'People', politicians and populism. *Government and Opposition*, 19, 312–27.

Canovan, M. 1990: On being economical with the truth: some liberal reflections. *Political Studies*, 38, 5–19.

Canovan, M. 1996: *Nationhood and Political Theory*. Cheltenham: Edward Elgar.

Canovan, M. 1998: Crusaders, sceptics and the nation. *Journal of Political Ideologies*, 3, 237–53.

Canovan, M. 1999: Trust the People! Populism and the two faces of democracy. *Political Studies*, 47, 2–16.

Canovan, M. 2000: Patriotism is not enough. *British Journal of Political Science*, 30, 413–32.

Canovan, M. 2002a: Taking politics to the people: populism as the ideology of democracy. In Y. Mény and Y. Surel (eds), *Democracies and the Populist Challenge*. Basingstoke: Palgrave, 25–44.

Canovan, M. 2002b: Democracy and nationalism. In A. Carter and G. Stokes (eds), *Democratic Theory Today*. Cambridge: Polity, 149–70.

Canovan, M. 2002c: The people, the masses, and the mobilization of power: the paradox of Hannah Arendt's 'populism'. *Social Research*, 69, 187–206.

Canovan, M. 2004: Populism for political theorists? *Journal of Political Ideologies*, 9, 241–52.

Carter, A. 2001: *The Political Theory of Global Citizenship*. London: Routledge.

Cassese, A. 1995: *Self-determination of Peoples: a Legal Reappraisal*. Cambridge: Cambridge University Press.

Chesterton, G. K. 1933: *Collected Poems*. London: Methuen.

Cicero 1999: *On the Commonwealth*, ed. J. E. G. Zetzel. Cambridge: Cambridge University Press.

Cohen, J. 1997: Deliberation and democratic legitimacy. In J. Bohman and W. Rehg (eds), *Deliberative Democracy: Essays on Reason and Politics*. Cambridge, Mass.: MIT Press, 67–91.

Cohen, J. 1998: Democracy and liberty. In J. Elster (ed.), *Deliberative Democracy*, Cambridge: Cambridge University Press, 185–231.

Cole, G. D. H. 1948: *A History of the Labour Party from 1914*. London: Routledge and Kegan Paul.

Commager, H. S. (ed.) 1949: *Documents of American History*, 5th edn. New York: Appleton-Century-Crofts.

Commager, H. S. (ed.) 1951: *Living Ideas in America*. New York: Harper and Bros.

Crook, D. P. 1965: *American Democracy in English Politics, 1815–1850*. Oxford: Oxford University Press.

Dahrendorf, R. 1990: *Reflections on the Revolution in Europe*. London: Chatto and Windus.

Della Porte, D. and Diani, M. 1999: *Social Movements: an Introduction*. Oxford: Blackwell.

Derathé, R. 1950: *Jean-Jacques Rousseau et la Science Politique de son Temps*. Paris: Presses Universitaires de France.

Di Tella, 1997: Populism into the twenty-first century. *Government and Opposition*, 32, 187–200.

Dornbusch, R. and Edwards S. 1990: Macroeconomic populism. *Journal of Development Economics*, 32, 247–77.

Dryzek, J. S. 2000: *Deliberative Democracy and Beyond: Liberals, Critics, Contestations*. Oxford: Oxford University Press.

Dufour, A. 1991: Pufendorf. In J. H. Burns with M. Goldie (eds), *The Cambridge History of Political Thought, 1450–1700*. Cambridge: Cambridge University Press, 561–88.

Dunbabin, J. 1988: Government (*c*.1150–1450). In J. H. Burns (ed.), *The Cambridge History of Medieval Political Thought, c.350–1450*. Cambridge: Cambridge University Press, 477–519.

Elster, J. (ed.) 1998: *Deliberative Democracy*. Cambridge: Cambridge University Press.

Epstein, J. A. 1994: *Radical Expression: Political Language, Ritual and Symbol in England, 1790–1850*. Oxford: Oxford University Press.

Feldherr, A. 1998: *Spectacle and Society in Livy's History*. Berkeley: University of California Press.

Filmer, Sir R. 1949: *Patriarcha and other Political Writings*, ed. P. Laslett. Oxford: Basil Blackwell.

Finley, M. I. 1983: *Politics in the Ancient World*. Cambridge: Cambridge University Press.

Fishkin, J. 1991: *Democracy and Deliberation: New Directions for Democratic Reform*. New Haven: Yale University Press.

Fishkin, J. 1995: *The Voice of the People: Public Opinion and Democracy*. New Haven: Yale University Press.

Folz, R. 1974: *The Coronation of Charlemagne*. London: Routledge and Kegan Paul.

Foote, G. 1985: *The Labour Party's Political Thought: a History*. London: Croom Helm.

Fortescue, Sir J. 1997: *On the Laws and Governance of England*, ed. S. Lockwood. Cambridge: Cambridge University Press.

Franklin, J. H. 1978: *John Locke and the Theory of Sovereignty*. Cambridge: Cambridge University Press.

Franklin, M. N., Van der Eijk, C. and Marsh, M. 1995: Referendum outcomes and trust in government: public support for Europe in the wake of Maastricht. In J. Hayward (ed.), *The Crisis of Representation in Europe*. London: Frank Cass, 101–17.

Freeden, M. 1996: *Ideologies and Political Theory: a Conceptual Approach*. Oxford: Clarendon Press.

Gallagher, M. and Uleri, P. V. (eds) 1996: *The Referendum Experience in Europe*. London: Macmillan.

Garton Ash, T. 1990: *We The People: the Revolution of 1989 Witnessed in Warsaw, Budapest, Berlin and Prague*. Cambridge: Granta.

Gierke, O. 1950: *Natural Law and the Theory of Society 1500–1800*, ed. E. Barker. Boston: Beacon Press.

Gilbert, M. (ed.) 1968: *Lloyd George*. Englewood Cliffs, NJ: Prentice Hall.

Goldie, M. 1980: The roots of True Whiggism 1688–94. *History of Political Thought*, 1, 195–236.

Goldsworthy, J. 1999: *The Sovereignty of Parliament: History and Philosophy*. Oxford: Oxford University Press.

Goodwyn, L. 1976: *Democratic Promise: the Populist Moment in America*. New York: Oxford University Press.

Goodwyn, L. 1991: *Breaking the Barrier: the Rise of Solidarity in Poland*. New York: Oxford University Press.

Gordon, T. 1737: *The Works of Tacitus, with Political Discourses*. London.

Gough, J. W. 1936: *The Social Contract*. Oxford: Oxford University Press.

Greenfeld, L. 1992: *Nationalism: Five Roads to Modernity*. Cambridge, Mass.: Harvard University Press.

Grimm, D. 1995: Does Europe need a constitution? *European Law Journal*, 1, 282–302.

Habermas, J. 1994: Three normative models of democracy. *Constellations*, 1, 1–10.

Habermas, J. 1995: Remarks on Dieter Grimm's 'Does Europe need a constitution?'. *European Law Journal*, 1, 303–07.

Habermas, J. 1996a: Citizenship and national identity. In J. Habermas, *Between Facts and Norms: Contributions to a Discourse Theory of Law and Democracy*. Cambridge, Mass.: MIT Press.

Habermas, J. 1996b: Popular sovereignty as procedure. In J. Habermas, *Between Facts and Norms: Contributions to a Discourse Theory of Law and Democracy*. Cambridge, Mass.: MIT Press.

Habermas, J. 1999: The European nation-state and the pressures of globalization. *New Left Review*, 235, 46–59.

Habermas, J. 2001: Why Europe needs a constitution. *New Left Review*, second series, 11, 5–26.

Haider, J. 1995: *The Freedom I Mean*. Pine Plains, NY: Swan Books.

Hallis, F. 1930: *Corporate Personality: a Study in Jurisprudence*. London: Oxford University Press.

Hamilton, A., Jay, J. and Madison, J. 1886: *The Federalist: a Commentary on the Constitution of the United States*. London: T. Fisher Unwin.

Hayward, J. (ed.) 1995: *The Crisis of Representation in Europe*. London: Frank Cass.

Hazlitt, W. 1991: *Selected Writings*, ed. J. Crook. Oxford: Oxford University Press.

Hicks, J. D. 1961: *The Populist Revolt*. Lincoln: University of Nebraska Press.

Hill, C. 1968: The Norman Yoke. In C. Hill, *Puritanism and Revolution*, London: Panther Books, 58–125.

Hill, C. 1974: The many-headed monster. In C. Hill, *Change and Continuity in Seventeenth-Century England*, London, Weidenfeld and Nicolson, 181–204.

Hobbes, T. 1960: *Leviathan*, ed. M. Oakeshott. Oxford: Basil Blackwell.

Hobbes, T. 1983: *De Cive*, ed. H. Warrender. Oxford: Clarendon Press.

Hofstadter, R. 1964: *Anti-Intellectualism in American Life*. London: Jonathan Cape.

Hofstadter, R. 1968: *The Age of Reform: From Bryan to F. D. R.* New York: Alfred A. Knopf.

Holden, B. 1993: *Understanding Liberal Democracy*, 2nd edn. New York: Harvester Wheatsheaf.

Holden, B. (ed.) 2000: *Global Democracy: Key Debates*. London: Routledge.

Holmes, S. 1995: *Passions and Constraints: on the Theory of Liberal Democracy*. Chicago: University of Chicago Press.

Holton, S. S. 1986: *Feminism and Democracy: Women's Suffrage and Reform Politics in Britain, 1900–1918*. Cambridge: Cambridge University Press.

Homo, L. 1929: *Roman Political Institutions from City to State*. London: Kegan Paul, Trench, Trubner.

Hont, I. 1994: The permanent crisis of a divided mankind: 'Contemporary crisis of the nation state' in historical perspective. *Political Studies*, 42, Special Issue, 166–231.

Horace 1994: *Epistles*, Book I, ed. R. Mayer. Cambridge: Cambridge University Press.

Hutchings, K. and Dannreuther, R. (eds) 1999: *Cosmopolitan Citizenship*. Basingstoke: Macmillan.

Immerfall, S. 1998: Conclusion: the neo-populist agenda. In H-G. Betz and S. Immerfall (eds), *The New Politics of the Right: Neo-Populist Parties and Movements in Established Democracies*. London: Macmillan, 249–61.

Ionescu, G. and Gellner, E. (eds) 1969: *Populism: its Meanings and National Characteristics*. London: Weidenfeld and Nicholson.

Jackson, R. 1999: 'Introduction: sovereignty at the millennium', *Political Studies*, 47, Special Issue, 423–56.

Johannsen, R. W. (ed.) 1965: *The Union in Crisis, 1850–1877*. New York: The Free Press.

Joyce, P. 1991: *Visions of the People: Industrial England and the Question of Class, 1848–1914*. Cambridge: Cambridge University Press.

Joyce, P. 1994: *Democratic Subjects: the Self and the Social in Nineteenth-Century England*. Cambridge: Cambridge University Press.

Kantorowicz, E. 1957: *The King's Two Bodies: a Study in Medieval Political Theology*. Princeton: Princeton University Press.

Kazin, M. 1995: *The Populist Persuasion: an American History*. New York: Basic Books.

Kingdom, R. M. 1991: Calvinism and resistance theory, 1550–1580. In J. H. Burns with M. Goldie (eds), *The Cambridge History of Political Thought, 1450–1700*. Cambridge: Cambridge University Press, 193–218.

Knight, J. and Johnson, J. 1994: Aggregation and deliberation: on the possibility of democratic legitimacy. *Political Theory*, 22, 277–96.

Kobach, K. W. 1993: *The Referendum: Direct Democracy in Switzerland*. Aldershot: Dartmouth.

Koselleck, R. 1985: *Futures Past*, ed. K. Tribe. Cambridge, Mass.: MIT Press.

Kymlicka, W. 1995: *Multicultural Citizenship*. Oxford: Oxford University Press.

Laba, R. 1991: *The Roots of Solidarity: a Political Sociology of Poland's Working-Class Democratization*. Princeton: Princeton University Press.

Laclau, E. 1979: *Politics and Ideology in Marxist Theory – Capitalism – Fascism – Populism*. London: Verso.

Laclau, E. 2005: Populism: what's in a name? In F. Panizza (ed.) *Populism and the Mirror of Democracy*. London: Verso, 32–49.

Lawson, G. 1992: *Politica Sacra et Civilis*. Cambridge: Cambridge University Press.

Lefort, C. 1986: *The Political Forms of Modern Society: Bureaucracy, Democracy, Totalitarianism*. Cambridge: Polity.

Linder, W. 1994: *Swiss Democracy: Possible Solutions to Conflict in Multicultural Societies*. New York: St. Martin's Press.

Linklater, A. 1998: *The Transformation of Political Community*. Cambridge: Polity.

Linklater, A. 1999: Cosmopolitan citizenship. In K. Hutchings and R. Dannreuther (eds) *Cosmopolitan Citizenship*, Basingstoke: Macmillan, 35–59.

Lintott, A. 1999: *The Constitution of the Roman Republic*. Oxford: Oxford University Press.

Lipset, S. M. and Raab, E. 1971: *The Politics of Unreason: Right-Wing Extremism in America, 1790–1970*. London: Heinemann.

Livius, T. 1974: *Ab Urbe Condita*, Vol. I. Oxford: Clarendon Press.

Locke, J. 1964: *Two Treatises of Government*, ed. P. Laslett. Cambridge: Cambridge University Press.

Lovett, W. and Collins, J. 1969: *Chartism: a New Organization of the People*. New York: Humanities Press.

Machiavelli, N. 1970: *The Discourses*, ed. B. Crick. Harmondsworth: Penguin.

Mack, M. P. (ed.) 1969: *A Bentham Reader*. New York: Pegasus.

Magleby, D. B. 1984: *Direct Legislation: Voting on Ballot Propositions in the United States*. Baltimore: Johns Hopkins University Press.

Mair, P. 2002: Populist democracy versus party democracy. In Y. Mény and Y. Surel (eds), *Democracies and the Populist Challenge*, Basingstoke: Palgrave, 81–98.

Manin, B. 1987: On legitimacy and political deliberation. *Political Theory*, 15, 338–68.

Manin, B. 1997: *The Principles of Representative Government*. Cambridge: Cambridge University Press.

Manning, P. 1992: *The New Canada*. Toronto: Macmillan.

Marcus, J. 1995: *The National Front and French Politics*. London: Macmillan.

Marshall, J. 1994: *John Locke: Resistance, Religion and Responsibility*. Cambridge: Cambridge University Press.

McLean, I. 1989: *Democracy and New Technology*. Cambridge: Polity.

McMath, R. C. 1993: *American Populism: a Social History 1877–1898*. New York: Hill and Wang.

Mény, Y. and Surel, Y. 2000: *Par le peuple, pour le people: le populisme et les démocraties*. Paris: Fayard.

Mény, Y. and Surel, Y. (eds) 2002: *Democracies and the Populist Challenge*. Basingstoke: Palgrave.

Michelet, J. 1967: *History of the French Revolution*. Chicago: University of Chicago Press.

Michelman, F. I. 1997: How can the people ever make the laws? A critique of deliberative democracy. In J. Bohman and W. Rehg (eds): *Deliberative Democracy: Essays on Reason and Politics*. Cambridge, Mass.: MIT Press: 145–71.

Mill, J. S. 1962: *Considerations on Representative Government*. Chicago: Henry Regnery.

Millar, F. 1998: *The Crowd in Rome in the Late Republic*. Ann Arbor: University of Michigan Press.

Millar, F. 2002: *The Roman Republic in Political Thought*. Brandeis: University Press of New England.

Miller, D. 1993: Deliberative democracy and social choice. In D. Held (ed.) *Prospects for Democracy: North, South, East, West*. Cambridge: Polity, 74–92.

Miller, D. 1999: Bounded citizenship. In K. Hutchings and R. Dannreuther (eds), *Cosmopolitan Citizenship*. Basingstoke: Macmillan, 60–80.

Morgan, E. 1988: *Inventing the People: the Rise of Popular Sovereignty in England and America*. New York: W. W. Norton.

Mudde, C. 2002: In the name of the peasantry, the proletariat, and the people: populisms in Eastern Europe. In Y. Mény and Y. Surel (eds), *Democracies and the Populist Challenge*. Basingstoke: Palgrave, 214–32.

Müller, W. 2002: Evil or the 'engine of democracy'? Populism and party competition in Austria. In Y. Mény and Y. Surel (eds), *Democracies and the Populist Challenge*. Basingstoke: Palgrave, 155–75.

Musgrave, T. D. 1997: *Self-determination and National Minorities*. Oxford: Oxford University Press.

Nussbaum, M. et al. 1996: *For Love of Country: Debating the Limits of Patriotism*. Boston, Mass.: Beacon Press.

Oakeshott, M. 1996: *The Politics of Faith and the Politics of Scepticism*. New Haven: Yale University Press.

O'Brien, C. C. 1988: *God Land: Reflections on Religion and Nationalism*. Cambridge, Mass.: Harvard University Press.

Oldfield, A. 1990: *Citizenship and Community: Civic Republicanism and the Modern World*. London: Routledge.

Orwell, G. 1941: *The Lion and the Unicorn: Socialism and the English Genius*. London: Secker and Warburg.

Paine, T. 1989: *Political Writings*, ed. B. Kuklick. Cambridge: Cambridge University Press.

Palmer, R. R. 1959: *The Age of the Democratic Revolution*, Vol. I. Princeton: Princeton University Press.

Pitkin, H. 1967: *The Concept of Representation*. Berkeley: University of California Press.

Pocock, J. G. A. 1975: *The Machiavellian Moment: Florentine Political Thought and the Atlantic Republican Tradition*. Princeton: Princeton University Press.

Pocock, J. G. A. 1987: The concept of a language and the *métier d'historien*. In A. Pagden (ed.), *The Languages of Political Theory in Early-Modern Europe*. Cambridge: Cambridge University Press.

Pocock, J. G. A. 1992: Introduction. In J. Harrington, *The Commonwealth of Oceana and A System of Politics*. Cambridge: Cambridge University Press.

Pole, J. R. 1978: *The Pursuit of Equality in American History*. Berkeley: University of California Press.

Pollack, N. (ed.), 1967: *The Populist Mind*. Indianapolis: Bobbs–Merrill.

Pufendorf, S. 1717: *Of the Law of Nature and Nations*. London: printed for R. Sare et al.

Rahe, P. 1992: *Republics Ancient and Modern: Classical Republicanism and the American Revolution*. Chapel Hill: University of North Carolina Press.

Rawls, J. 1972: *A Theory of Justice*. Oxford: Oxford University Press.

Reich, J. 1990: Reflections on becoming an East German dissident, on losing the Wall and a country. In G. Prins (ed.), *Spring in Winter: the 1989 Revolutions*. Manchester: Manchester University Press, 65–97.

Reid, J. P. 1989: *The Concept of Representation in the Age of the American Revolution*. Chicago: Chicago University Press.

Reynolds, S. 1984: *Kingdoms and Communities in Western Europe, 900–1300*. Oxford; Oxford University Press.

Reynolds, S. 1995: *Ideas and Solidarities of the Medieval Laity*. Aldershot: Variorum.

Richardson, H. S. 1997: Democratic intentions. In J. Bohman and W. Rehg (eds), *Deliberative Democracy: Essays on Reason and Politics*. Cambridge, Mass.: MIT Press, 349–82.

Riker, W. 1982: *Liberalism Against Populism: a Confrontation Between the Theory of Democracy and the Theory of Social Choice*. San Francisco: W. H. Freeman.

Robbins, C. 1959: *The Eighteenth-century Commonwealthman*. Cambridge, Mass.: Harvard University Press.

Rousseau, J. J. 1911: *Emile*. London: Dent.

Rousseau, J. J. 1962: *The Political Writings*, 2 volumes, ed. C. E. Vaughan. Oxford: Basil Blackwell.

Rousseau, J. J. 1987: On the Social Contract. In J. J. Rousseau, *Basic Political Writings*, ed. D. A. Cress. Indianapolis: Hackett.

Salmon, J. H. M. 1991: Catholic resistance theory, Ultramontanism, and the royalist response, 1580–1620. In J. H. Burns with M. Goldie (eds), *The Cambridge History of Political Thought, 1450–1700*. Cambridge: Cambridge University Press, 218–53.

Sartori, G. 1962: *Democratic Theory*. Detroit: Wayne State University Press.

Saward, M. 1998: *The Terms of Democracy*. Cambridge: Polity.

Schaar, J. H. 1981: *Legitimacy in the Modern State*. New Brunswick: Transaction.

Schnapper, D. 1994: *La communauté des citoyens: sur l'idée moderne de la nation*. Paris: Gallimard.

Schöpflin, G. 1997: The function of myth and a taxonomy of myth. In G. Hosking and G. Schöpflin (eds), *Myth and Nationhood*. London: Hurst, 19–37.

Shakespeare, W. 1967: *Coriolanus*. London: Penguin Books.

Sharp, A. (ed.) 1998: *The English Levellers*. Cambridge: Cambridge University Press.

Shils, E. 1956: *The Torment of Secrecy*. London: William Heinemann.

Skinner, Q. 1978: *The Foundations of Modern Political Thought*. Cambridge: Cambridge University Press.

Smith, G. 1976: The functional properties of the referendum. *European Journal of Political Research*, 4, 1–23.

Smith, R. M. 2003: *Stories of Peoplehood: the Politics and Morals of Political Membership*. Cambridge: Cambridge University Press.

Sorel, G. 1950: *Reflections on Violence*. New York and London: Macmillan.

Stedman Jones, G. 1983: *Languages of Class: Studies in English Working Class History, 1832–1982*. Cambridge, Cambridge University Press.

Surel, Y. 2002: Populism in the French party system. In Y. Mény and Y. Surel (eds), *Democracies and the Populist Challenge*. Basingstoke: Palgrave, 139–54.

Taggart, P. 1995: New populist parties in Western Europe. *West European Politics*, 18, 34–51.

Taggart, P. 2000: *Populism*. Buckingham: Open University Press.

Taggart, P. 2002: Populism and the pathology of representative politics. In Y. Mény and Y. Surel (eds), *Democracies and the Populist Challenge*. Basingstoke: Palgrave, 62–80.

Talmon, J. L. 1952: *The Origins of Totalitarian Democracy*. London: Secker and Warburg.

Tarchi, M. 2002: Populism Italian style. In Y. Mény and Y. Surel (eds), *Democracies and the Populist Challenge*. Basingstoke: Palgrave, 120–38.

Telos 1991: K. Anderson, R. A. Berman, T. Luke, P. Piccone and M. Taves, 'The empire strikes out: a roundtable on populist politics', No. 87, 3–37; *Telos* staff: 'Populism vs. the New Class', No. 88, 2–36. New York.

The Economist, 27 April 2002: After the cataclysm. London, 25–7.

The Economist, 4 May 2002: Political games. London, 14–16.

Thom, M. 1995: *Republics, Nations and Tribes*. London: Verso.

Thompson, E. P. 1963: *The Making of the English Working Class*. London: Victor Gollancz.

Tierney, B. 1982: *Religion, Law, and the Growth of Constitutional Thought, 1150–1650*. Cambridge: Cambridge University Press.

Tocqueville, A. de, 1862: *Democracy in America*, trans. H. Reeve, 2 vols. London: Longman, Green, Longman, and Roberts.

Touraine, A., Dubet, F., Wieviorka, M. and Strzelecki, J., et al. 1983: *Solidarity: the Analysis of a Social Movement*. Cambridge: Cambridge University Press.

Tuck, R. 1979: *Natural Rights Theories: Their Origin and Development*. Cambridge: Cambridge University Press.

Tuck, R. 1991: Grotius and Selden. In J. H. Burns with M. Goldie (eds), *The Cambridge History of Political Thought, 1450–1700*. Cambridge: Cambridge University Press, 499–529.

Tudor, H. 1972: *Political Myth*. London: Pall Mall.

Tymowski, A. W. 1991–2: Workers vs. intellectuals in *Solidarnosc*. *Telos*, 90, 157–74.

Ullmann, W. 1965: *A History of Political Thought in the Middle Ages*. Harmondsworth: Penguin.

Venturi, F. 1960: *The Roots of Revolution*. London: Weidenfeld and Nicholson.

Viroli, M. 1995: *For Love of Country: an Essay on Patriotism and Nationalism*. Oxford: Oxford University Press.

Walker, R. B. J. 1999: Citizenship after the modern subject. In K. Hutchings and R. Dannreuther (eds), *Cosmopolitan Citizenship*. Basingstoke: Macmillan, 171–200.

Ware, A. 2002: The United States: populism as political strategy. In Y. Mény and Y. Surel (eds), *Democracies and the Populist Challenge*. Basingstoke: Palgrave, 101–19.

Warren, M. 2002: Deliberative democracy. In A. Carter and G. Stokes (eds), *Democratic Theory Today*. Cambridge: Polity, 173–202.

Weale, A. 1999: *Democracy*. London: Macmillan.

Weiler, J. H. H. 1995: Does Europe need a constitution? *Demos, Telos* and the German Maastricht decision. *European Law Journal*, 1: 219–58.

Westlind, D. 1996: *The Politics of Popular Identity: Understanding Recent Populist Movements in Sweden and the United States*. Lund: Lund University Press.

Whelan, F. G. 1983: Democratic theory and the boundary problem. In J. R. Pennock and J. W. Chapman (eds), *Liberal Democracy*, Nomos 25. New York: New York University Press, 13–42.

Wolin, S. 1994: Fugitive democracy. *Constellations*, 1, 11–25.

Wood, G. S. 1992: *The Radicalism of the American Revolution*. New York: Alfred A. Knopf.

Wootton, D. (ed.) 1986: *Divine Right and Democracy: an Anthology of Political Writing in Stuart England*. London: Penguin.

Wootton, D. 1991: Leveller democracy and the Puritan Revolution. In J. H. Burns with M.Goldie (eds), *The Cambridge History of Political Thought, 1450–1700*. Cambridge: Cambridge University Press, 412–42.

Wootton, D. 1993: Introduction. In J. Locke, *Political Writings*, ed. D. Wootton. London; Penguin.

Wortman, R. 1967: *The Crisis of Russian Populism*. Cambridge: Cambridge University Press.

Yack, B. 1996: The myth of the civic nation. *Critical Review*, 10: 193–211.

Yack, B. 2001: Popular sovereignty and nationalism. *Political Theory*, 29: 517–36.

Yack, B. (forthcoming) *Nation and Individual: Contingency, Choice and Community in Modern Political Life*.

Index

CPSIA information can be obtained
at www.ICGtesting.com
Printed in the USA
BVOW06s2100250817
492806BV00010B/39/P